D0931653

Please return or renew by
latest date below

**LOANS MAY BE RENEWED BY PHONE**
648-571°

# The economics
# and politics of socialism

By the same author

The market in a socialist economy *(1972)*

# The economics and politics of socialism

## Collected essays

**Włodzimierz Brus**

With a Foreword by Maurice Dobb

Routledge & Kegan Paul
London and Boston

*First published in 1973*
*by Routledge & Kegan Paul Ltd*
*Broadway House, 68–74 Carter Lane,*
*London EC4V 5EL and*
*9 Park Street,*
*Boston, Mass. 02108, U.S.A.*

*Chapters 3–6 translated by Angus Walker,*
*revised by the author*

*Printed in Great Britain by*
*Butler & Tanner Ltd, Frome and London*

*ISBN 0 7100 7474 3*

*Library of Congress Catalog Number 73-77037*

# Contents

# Foreword
## by Maurice Dobb

Professor Włodzimierz Brus became known to us, here as elsewhere, as having contributed important new ideas and a novel viewpoint to the debate about the role of the market in a planned economy as a result, first, of a short book of 1956, *Prawo wartości a problematyka bodzców ekonomicznych* (*The Law of Value and the Problem of Economic Incentives*), and, second, in 1961, of a broader work entitled *Ogólne problemy funkcjonowania gospodarki socjalistycznej* (*General Questions of the Functioning of a Socialist Economy*).[1] This latter drew upon the experience of socialist planning in the light of three important theoretical debates on a socialist economy: namely, discussion in the Soviet Union in the middle twenties, the controversy about economic calculation under socialism in the thirties and the debates of the middle fifties, especially in Poland, in the period following Stalin's death.

The present collection of articles and essays has an interest, however, that extends beyond the circle of those concerned with problems associated with the 'economic reforms' of the past decade in the planned economies of Eastern Europe. Some of the articles below bear upon the latter. But they are concerned also (as is, indeed, emphasized by the author) with wider political issues connected with the discussions, alike among Marxists in those countries and in the West, since the death of Stalin and especially since 1956: in particular, the question of democratization both within industry and also politically. Most readers will, I think, be struck by the frankness, indeed fearlessness, as well as the clarity and balance with which such questions are formulated and discussed—an outspokenness that has been rather rare previously in discussion of this type.

At the time of his first book the author was about to become,

[1] Both of these works were published in Warsaw by P.W.N., and the second of them is available in English (*The market in a socialist economy*, Routledge & Kegan Paul, 1972).

almost simultaneously, Professor of Economics at Warsaw University, head of the department of economic research of the Planning Commission and Vice-Chairman of the State Economic Council from 1956 to 1962. In these capacities he was a close colleague of the late Professor Oskar Lange; and he also collaborated with that other famous Polish economist, Michał Kalecki, in drafting certain initiating documents of the Polish Economic Reform of 1956–7 (adopted in principle by the government at the time but never put into effective and full operation). He speaks accordingly with some experience of problems of planning and economic administration, and not only as a theorist. Up to 1956, after being a student of economics at the Free University of Warsaw before the war and spending most of the war years in the Soviet Union, he had successively studied and lectured at the Warsaw High School of Planning and Statistics (where both Lange and Kalecki also taught for a time); he had also held the chair of political economy at the Institute of Social Sciences attached to the Central Committee of the Polish Workers' Party during the first half of the fifties. From 1968 he was employed as a research worker at the Institute of Housing Economy, and is at present on a visit to the University of Glasgow.

It is not easy to single out any particular sections or ideas in this collection for special mention. But if one were to try to do so, perhaps one would draw the attention of English readers to the following as specially deserving consideration and discussion. First, there is his notion of 'socialization of the means of production as a *process*', not an initial once-for-all act; with the implied need for a subsequent progressive 'deepening of its social character—a development connected with the whole of the economic relations between people' (in which context come some pointed comments on Djilas and on Rosa Luxemburg). Second, his treatment of issues connected with decentralization, which comes into chapter 4, also chapter 3, as well as explicitly in chapter 1. Third, his emphasis, especially in chapter 5, upon the interpenetration of economic and political decisions in socialist planning ('the tendency at various times and for various reasons to eliminate one of the terms from political economy must be resisted'). Finally, his illuminating (if possibly controversial) analysis of the Polish events of December 1970, translated from the Italian weekly *Rinascita*. One can certainly congratulate alike author, translators and publisher upon the appearance of this collection in English.

# 1 | Some general problems of decentralization in a socialist planned economy[1]

For at least ten years the questions of development of the system of functioning of the planned economy constituted in Poland the subject of broad and lively discussions. Both aspects, purely theoretical and practical, are quite comprehensively represented. After reaching something like a climax in the years 1956–8, the discussion subsided for a while but came again to the forefront in the last two years. Necessary changes in the system of functioning of the socialist planned economy belong now to the top priority socio-economic questions. This is true not only of Poland but, to a lesser or higher degree, true also of other Eastern European socialist countries, including the Soviet Union.

The fact that questions posed for discussion are not losing their importance over time seems to show that the need for some institutional changes in the functioning system of a planned economy stems from the very realities of the economic life.

The overall balance of the twenty-year experience of the socialist planned economy in Poland is evidently favourable. Poland belongs to the group of countries with a very high average rate of growth of the national income. The scale of social and economic transformations accomplished during this relatively short historical period is enormous. Taking into account the extremely heavy war losses, the overall favourable picture becomes even more distinct, particularly in comparison both with pre-war Poland and many other countries which started after World War II from a similar level of development.

However, this does not mean that the Polish experience, and the experience of other socialist countries as well, does not give reasons

[1] This paper was published in German under the title *Die Entwicklung des sozialistischen Wirtschaftssystems in Polen. Bemerkungen zu einigen allgemeinen Problemen* (Hamburger Jahrbuch für Wirtschafts- und Gesellschaftspolitik, 1965). It contains large excerpts from a paper, '*Problems of decentralization in a socialist planned economy*', presented by the author at the Sixth World Congress of the International Political Science Association, Geneva, 1964.

for critical analysis with regard to those concrete institutional forms which are at present used in our system of planned economy. When relating potential possibilities to the actual performance, there is much scope for deliberation. At first, the causes of some negative phenomena were sought primarily in subjective factors dependent upon the way of action of different chains of command in the economy. Certainly such factors always have some importance. A closer analysis, however, showed quite soon that, apart from the subjective side, significant institutional factors had to be taken into account.

Gradually the view emerged that the general principles of socialist planned economy could be attained not only through a single institutional form, established once for ever, but—within a definite framework, of course—through different forms. This is particularly true when different conditions of various economies and various levels of development are taken into consideration. The idea of the possibility of implementing different institutional solutions within the framework of a planned economy posed many basic questions usually reduced to the scope of centralization and decentralization of economic decision-making. This approach could be accepted under the condition, however, that not only the purely organizational aspect is considered, but—and on a full scale—also the economic side, first of all the interrelations between plan and market mechanism.

The emergence of these sorts of problems in conjunction with some practical attempts at new solutions raised a wave of interest not only in socialist countries but also in the capitalist world. In Western literature, particularly in that of a more journalistic nature, the interpretation was not always the correct one. Attempts were made to present this discussion as a signal for retreat from planned economy as such, whereas in reality the effort was concentrated on improving the way of operation of the planned economy.

The present article is an attempt to depict the main issues raised in the course of the Polish discussion. However, the author does not intend to give a review but to present the problems from his own point of view. It goes without saying that the present writer's approach may be disputed by many participants in the Polish discussion, not only with regard to details but with regard to some basic assumptions as well. The reader should be also aware that for obvious reasons problems are presented here in the form of an outline rather than a comprehensive analysis.

## The real scope of centralization versus decentralization problem in a socialist economy

The relation between centralized and decentralized decisions in the course of planning and execution of plans will be looked upon here not regionally but from what might be called sectoral decentralization, i.e., national economy, industry, branch, enterprise. For the sake of simplicity the intermediate stages will be left out and only the relation 'central level–enterprise' will be discussed. It is to be noticed, however, that not only a single establishment but also a large association may be included under the heading 'enterprise'.

It seems necessary to begin with a delimination of the scope within which discussion of centralization and decentralization in a socialist economy is valid at all. We assume here a fully socialized economy: all means of production are in public (state) ownership, the sole source of individual income being work in public enterprises or institutions, apart from social benefits or similar budget payments—pensions, scholarships, disability compensations, etc. In one point only will this assumption be modified and some remarks concerning small-scale private production, predominantly farming, included.

By definition a socialist economy requires centralization of at least some kinds of decisions. A central level of economic decision-taking, a 'headquarters', is an indispensable feature of such an economy. The central level acts according to certain specific ends and criteria of activity. We assume, and this stems from the author's understanding of the essence of a socialist economy, that these ends and criteria should conform with the public interest. The economic calculus on which the central decisions are based is thus of a macroeconomic nature, i.e., alternatives are considered from the point of view of the national economy as a whole and not from the point of view of particular sectors, branches and enterprises. Another feature of economic calculus in socialism may be added—the predominance of dynamic and long-run criteria.

The economic calculus on the central level, as a basis for taking

3

the *main macro-economic decisions* has predominantly the features of the so-called 'direct calculus', i.e., a calculus which does not rest on the market criteria as the source of the basic data but deals in principle with physical magnitudes.[2] Such decisions as the determination of the long-run rate of growth and the closely linked decision about the share of productive investment in the national income, as the distribution of investment between various branches of the economy, in broad terms, and closely linked to it the question of the future structure of final product, again in broad terms, as the principles of distribution of the consumption fund, etc., are not and could not be taken in a socialist planned economy on the basis of the signals and criteria coming from the market. This is particularly true of perspective plans covering a period of fifteen to twenty years. This does not mean, however, that market or quasi-market criteria should be entirely ignored, especially taking into account the indispensable procedure of successive approximations, which assumes the necessity of corrections caused by feedbacks. In the course of taking the main macro-economic and long-run decisions, the market magnitudes, however, always play a secondary role compared with the primary element of direct confrontation of disposable resources and desirable effects along the generally accepted lines of development.[3] It is just from this point of view that the author thinks it necessary for any type of socialist planned economy, the Yugoslav type included, to maintain the superior position of the 'headquarters' with regard to all other components of the organizational structure. Hierarchical

[2] The terms 'direct calculus' and 'indirect calculus' (a calculus in market magnitudes either real or of a 'shadow market') were introduced into the Polish discussion by A. Wakar and J. G. Zieliński. See particularly Zieliński: *The Economic Calculus in Socialism in Connection with the Discussion on Economic Calculus in Socialism in Anglo-Saxon Literature*, Warsaw, 1961. These terms are at present quite widely used in Poland although many authors, including the present writer, do not share the theoretical corollaries drawn by A. Wakar and J. G. Zieliński from their distinction between direct and indirect calculus.

[3] For a very good description of some of the methods applied in Polish perspective planning, see M. Kalecki: 'Outline of a method of constructing a perspective plan' presented to the UN Conference on the Application of Science and Technology for the Benefit of the Less-developed Areas, Geneva, 1963.

4

relations and vertical links between higher and lower levels are indispensable in a planned economy which cannot rely merely on horizontal links established through the market.

However, this does not yet solve the problem of scope of centralization because it is not tantamount to stating that a planned economy must always centralize *all* decisions and operate *only* through vertical links.

First of all a very important sphere of *decisions made by individuals* (households) has to be taken into account. Included here are decisions concerning the choice of profession and place of work, along with the question of the so-called degree of activity in the working-process: improving skills, increasing labour-productivity, etc., and decisions concerning the choice of the consumer-goods basket. This sphere of decisions can be in some sense considered as the other extreme compared with the main macro-economic decisions. As a rule, the latter are taken on the central level; the former are as a rule made in a decentralized way. There are no reasons why, apart from obviously exceptional cases, the freedom of choice of profession and place of work and the freedom of choice concerning the structure of consumption should not be considered as an indispensable feature of the socialist economy. Thus, the general characteristics of any socialist economy must include some scope of decentralized decision-making. This has important consequences. The decentralization of the decisions taken by the individuals as employees and consumers requires the necessary application of market forms, at least with regard to this sphere. In some Western writings on the subject of socialist economy, the importance of labour and consumer-goods market is being belittled on the ground that the decisions of employees and consumers are in fact determined by the central decisions concerning the magnitude and structure of personal incomes, the demand for labour, supply of consumer goods, etc. This approach seems to be unjustified. First, even if really the dependence would be only one-sided, it would still have a tremendous importance for the freedom of action of particular individuals (households) because market forms would allow for individual diversification, even in a situation when the aggregates should be adapted to the previously given structure. But in reality it would be wrong to approach the problem

5

in question only in such a limited way. The freedom of choice of profession and place of work and the freedom of choice of individual consumption-pattern exerts through the market mechanism an inverse influence on the structure of the demand for labour and on the structure of final production and, therefore, on the macro-economic decisions, at least to the extent they can be made consistent with the superior pattern of social preferences.

However, the question of how strong the influence of the labour and consumer-goods market is on production depends not only on the interrelations between those markets and the sphere of the main macro-economic decisions, but also on the method of decision-making on the level which lies somehow in between the macro-economic and the individual spheres of decisions. Included here are such problems as the concretion of the general development pattern in short-term, e.g., yearly, plans as the output programme of particular branches and enterprises, as the detailed structure of inputs, sources of supply and direction of sales, concrete systems of remuneration, etc. Certainly, the solutions on this level are determined in general terms by the central macro-economic decisions. Still, in the framework of general given directions, considerable scope for choosing among many alternative courses of action remains. And this justifies, in the author's opinion, the separation of an intermediate group called frequently *current or sectoral decisions*. With regard to this group of decisions one cannot say beforehand whether they have to be made in a way analogous to the main macro-economic decisions, i.e., directly on the central level, or whether they should be left in the hands of the socialized enterprises, possibly including branch organizations under the heading 'enterprise'. In the latter case a new sphere of operation of the market mechanism emerges—that between the 'headquarters' and the enterprises. This leads also to considerable enhancement of the mutual interactions between the labour and consumer-goods market on the one hand and the market relations between socialized enterprises on the other.

Summing up this part of the discussion, one would say that the question of the scope of centralization *versus* decentralization in a socialist planned economy could be schematically approached by dividing all economic decisions into three groups:

1. basic macro-economic decisions which determine the general direction of economic development: the rate of growth of national income, the shares of investment and consumption in national income, the distribution of investment outlays between sectors and branches, the principles of distribution of the consumption fund between different social and vocational groups, etc.;

2. current (or sectional) decisions: the size and detailed structure of output of a given branch or enterprise, the sources of supplies and direction of sales, the structure of personnel and form and methods of remuneration inside a branch or an enterprise, etc.;

3. individual decisions: the composition of the consumer-goods basket in the framework of households income, the choice of profession and occupation, etc.

The dividing lines between the above groups of decisions are not always easy to draw, even theoretically. It is sufficient, however, from our point of view to grasp the general difference between the *types* of decisions included in each of the three groups. On this basis it is possible to define generally the limits of centralization and decentralization in a planned economy or, in other words, to determine *the minimum of* centralization on one hand and *the minimum of decentralization* on the other hand. Under the minimum of centralization, it is to be understood that in a socialist planned economy at least the first group of decisions, basic macro-decisions, must be taken by the central planner. At the other extreme, the minimum of decentralization consists of the decentralization of the third group of decisions. This does not mean that the central level is deprived of exerting influence on individual decisions; wide possibilities of such influence exist through determination of the parameters of individual choice (wages, prices, etc.). But this is an indirect form of influencing a decision which rests ultimately with an autonomous subject and differs substantially from taking the decision *for* him.

The scope of the 'centralization *versus* decentralization' problem in a planned economy is thus limited in principle to the second group of decisions, the current decisions, which occupy a somewhat intermediate position. They can be either centralized or decentralized, and, depending on the solution, we may distinguish two models of functioning of a planned economy: a centralized model and a decentralized model—strictly speaking, a model of the functioning of a planned economy with built-in market mechanism. The description of both models follows.

## The centralized model

Except for decisions contained in the third group, all other economic decisions (first group and second group) are taken in this model at the central level. In this sense the main feature of the centralistic model is (1) one-level decision-making. All other elements of the centralized model follow therefrom, namely (2) strictly hierarchical structure of the plans, plans of lower levels as formally subordinated sectors of the corresponding plans on the higher level, and predominance of the vertical links between central level and enterprises; horizontal links between enterprises themselves are of a purely technical, implementary character; (3) communications from the top to the bottom are transmitted in the form of direct *orders* which determine what has to be done and how (obligatory target-planning); communications from the bottom to the top can be called 'reports'; they supply material for the central decisions; (4) necessarily connected with this system of organization is the predominance of economic calculation and allocation of resources in physical terms; monetary forms do appear but their role is usually passive. Magnitudes expressed in money terms do not constitute the basis of choice, being merely an instrument of aggregation and control of fulfilment of the central decisions.

No concrete system of functioning of planned economy corresponds strictly to the centralized model described above. Only a more or less close approximation to this abstract description may be found. This 'gap' is due to many factors which prevent the attainment of a 100 per cent centralization in its strict sense. One has to remember, for example, that the 'processing capacity' of information into decisions of the central planner is limited, particularly at the present stage of development of the planning techniques; the result is that not all so-called central decisions are central decisions in fact: the 'headquarters' is simply unable to check all 'reports' and has recourse to rubber-stamping proposals and suggestions presented by the lower echelons. Furthermore, under the impact of incentives—in the broad sense both material and status questions—linked to the fulfilment of central targets, many informal organizational chains appear in economic relations, which cause the actual situation to deviate from the schematic picture given above.

Still, it would be wrong to consider the centralized model as invalid for an analysis of real forms of organization in a planned economy. One can easily discover operational systems of a planned economy based in principle on the centralized model. This was the case, for example, with the functioning of the Polish economy in the period 1949–55. Afterwards, some changes in the direction of decentralization were made. However, they did not go so far as to shift the system to one based on the assumption of a decentralized model.

## The decentralized model

The basic feature of this model in contradiction to the centralized one is the multiplicity of levels of decision-making. In our simplified case two levels of decision-making are considered: the central level (the first group of decisions) and the enterprise level (the second group of decisions). In a decentralized model plans on different levels are independently formulated: the central plan on the basis of the ends and standards of the 'headquarters', the plans of the enterprises on the basis of their 'rules of the game'. Thus, in this model the links between plans on different levels are achieved not by direct orders but by indirect means (economic instruments, see below). An important role is played here by horizontal links between enterprises themselves and hence by market relations; monetary means of allocation prevail.

Of course, the decentralized model must not impair the principle of superiority of the central plan. There is, however, an important question of methods. Generally speaking this superior position is achieved through a properly constructed set of general rules for the lower levels, the enterprises and a corresponding system of incentives steering the activity of the enterprises in the direction desirable from the point of view of the central level. Assuming, for example, that maximization of profit is the rule, the superior position of the central plan is based:

1. on the macro-economic character of direct central decisions, which determine the general conditions in which the enterprises are to work, e.g., the rate of increase of the productive capacity and its structure, the total demand and its structure, etc.;

2. on the appropriate use of instruments of economic policy, i.e., on the appropriate determination of market magnitudes, which serve as parameters of decisions taken by the enterprises (prices, wages, interest rates, taxation systems, etc.).

An enterprise, taking its autonomous decisions from the point of view of the general rules of behaviour, operates in a framework created by direct central decisions with regard to basic proportions and under the influence of centrally determined market magnitudes which serve as independent parameters for the enterprise's choice of product mix, structure of inputs, etc.

Obviously, the market mechanism plays an important role in the decentralized model. Monetary relations are active instruments in the operations of the economy, presenting real alternatives of choice and hence influencing the decisions of enterprises. This explains the use of the term 'model of functioning of a planned economy with built-in market mechanism' as more precise compared with the rather vague term 'decentralized model'.

The market mechanism in a decentralized model is endowed with at least two important features: (1) the market magnitudes must always preserve their parametric character in relation to the subject of choice and (2) the market magnitudes must be determined or at least effectively influenced in an indirect way by the central planner according to the public scale of preference. Hence, it is useful to call the market mechanism in this model a 'regulated market mechanism' in order to emphasize its role as an instrument of the plan and not as a spontaneous factor, independent of or even contradictory to planning. The task of building up such a mechanism is not an easy one. Problems have to be solved which were faced neither by classical capitalist economy, where the question of subordination of the market mechanism to previously accepted social ends did not arise at all, nor by the socialist economy based on the assumption of the centralistic model, where not the market mechanism but direct targets and physical allocation orders were employed.

Again we have to note that in practice principles of the decentralized model cannot be implemented without exceptions. Full replacement of the administrative system of management (planning by orders) by the parametric system of management (some call it the 'automated system') which is the key concept of the decentralized model encounters many difficulties. Even the Yugoslav system which is relatively close to the decentralized model makes use in some sectors of the administrative and not the parametric forms of management. In other socialist countries the system of obligatory target-planning still prevails, although in recent years a clear tendency towards the introduction of forms corresponding to the decentralized model can be observed.

It is here worth while to modify for a moment our assumption of a fully socialized economy and to mention the Polish experience with regard to the inclusion of agriculture in the planning system. Over 85 per cent of arable land is privately owned in Poland. Obviously so important a sector as agriculture, embracing more than one-third of the total active population, cannot remain outside the framework of the planned economy. On the other hand, individual farms cannot be included in the planning system by means of direct orders, as in the centralistic model. Hence, it is necessary to adopt methods of indirect steering by the state authorities, based on public ownership of the means of production outside agriculture and on a highly developed and diversified set of economic policy instruments, e.g., organization of purchase of agricultural products, supply of industrial means of production to agriculture, price policy, taxation policy, credit policy both with regard to working capital and to investments, etc. We do not consider as our task to give here a detailed description of the methods used; generally speaking, however, they are fairly effective from the standpoint of planning.

## The question of comparative effectiveness of the models

We are now facing the problem of weighing the relative effectiveness of the centralized and the decentralized model in a planned economy. It is not possible to make absolute judgments because the suitability of the first or the second solution, even taking into account that no pure solutions could be implemented, depends on many factors and concrete circumstances. What we shall try to do is to discuss the advantages and disadvantages of each concept in order to establish in what conditions each of them could and should prevail.

It emerges from our schematic description of the decentralized model that its aim is not decentralization in itself but the provision of a suitable means of attaining superior public ends, formulated at and achieved under the guidance of the central level, although with the use of methods different from those of the centralized model. Hence, an important question is sometimes advanced: why build up a complicated decentralized organization, steered by indirect means, when its ultimate task is to attain the ends of the 'headquarters' which is in a position to issue direct orders to lower echelons, obliging them to achieve those ends? Why choose, for example, a roundabout way of getting a change in the structure of production by means of price manipulations if the same effect is obtainable by direct order given to an enterprise?

The suggestions contained in the above questions could be accepted only when quite a complicated set of conditions is present, namely: (1) that the central level has a perfect knowledge of its own ends and is able to formulate them perfectly, i.e., not merely in general but in their detailed expression which is indispensable for creating a fully centralistic organization; (2) that the information flow through all necessary stages and in all directions, e.g., 'reports' from the bottom to the top, processing of 'reports' into decisions at the 'headquarters', communication of decisions to the bottom in the form of direct orders at a speed sufficient for reaching the executive stage without losing validity; (3) that information in the course of flowing in both directions and of processing does not undergo serious distortions, e.g., under the influence of particular interests governed by definite material and other motives.[4]

Obviously, these conditions can be met with a satisfactory degree of approximation only in particular circumstances. At least at the present stage of development of information techniques, they can be

[4] Cf. O. Lange: 'Niektóre zagadnienia centralizacji i decentralizacji w zarządzaniu' ('Some problems of centralization and decentralization in management'), *Materialy Prakseologiczne*, 1962.

more or less strictly fulfilled in a situation when only a relatively small number of paramount priorities is pursued. We leave aside the usually quoted examples of war objectives. But a concentration of resources on a given number of key projects in order to sharply raise the country's industrial capacity in a short time could serve as a good example.

In such conditions one of the main advantages of the centralistic model comes to the forefront—its *high selectivity*. By 'high selectivity' we understand the ability to direct means to strictly chosen priority sectors, leaving aside others, even closely related. This ability is connected with the method peculiar to the centralized model of determining targets and allocating resources in physical terms. Using this method it is possible, for example, to get not an increase in steel production in general, but an increase in a particular kind of steel production, to allocate this steel not for manufacturing in general, but for manufactures of a particular kind, etc., even though simultaneously unsatisfied demands for other sorts of steel and for other kinds of manufactures would exist. This essential feature of the centralistic model explains the tendency towards a high degree of centralization in some periods particularly in initial periods of rapid industrialization when violent changes in the structure of the economy occur, accompanied by disequilibria and tensions in many points (high targets *versus* very limited resources). Turning back to Polish conditions in the period of the Six Year Plan 1949–55, the then high degree of centralization was perhaps unjustified in all of its elements but to a given extent was undoubtedly determined by objective factors.

If one accepts, at least generally, the above line of reasoning, one can also easily answer the question about suitability of decentralization. With the economic targets growing more and more complex and the list of priorities broadening, the chances diminish of meeting conditions favouring the effective operation of a strictly centralized organization of a planned economy. An attempt at keeping such an organization alive without the conditions mentioned above may lead to diminishing efficiency in carrying out not only the second group of decisions but also the first group. For it is to be expected that the central level, under the heavy burden of growing current problems, may lose its ability to concentrate on main macro-economic questions. There is also a growing problem of adequacy of the signals received by the top echelons in a system virtually deprived of any significant role of the market in relations between socialist enterprises. As a result, the tendency towards a high degree of centralization for the sake of guaranteeing 'comprehensive planning' may turn out dangerous for the very foundations of planning and cause considerable losses.

With growing complexity of tasks and simultaneously growing diversity of disposable resources, there is a growing need:

—for flexibility in the process of adaptation to the needs of the product users;

—for the ability to substitute factors of production from the point of view of minimization of total outlays, as opposed to the 'quantity-of-output attitude' favoured in the centralized model;

—for the ability to promote technical innovations not only by key investment projects but also by opening the possibility of the enterprise's self-investment on a smaller scale, etc. With questions of this kind pushing their way to the forefront, the effectiveness of decentralization becomes enhanced. As has been said before, this decentralization does not mean giving up the planned management of the economy, but permits concentration on general problems, leaving the detailed decisions to the lower echelons, provided the latter act according to the rules and with the use of the parameters determined by the central level.

## Economic and socio-political side of the problem

Until now the problem of relative advantages of centralization and decentralization in a planned economy has been dealt with almost exclusively from a purely economic point of view. Obviously this is a too narrow approach. The problem 'centralization *versus* decentralization' in a planned economy has also its socio-political side, particularly from the point of view of factors contributing to the democratic way of development.

Some things are clear and need no further elaboration. Economic decentralization is, for example, an indispensable condition of workers' participation in management of nationalized enterprises, a condition of developing the necessary attitude of responsibility for public ownership, etc. The institution of workers' self-government in Poland came into being in close connection with some steps towards decentralization. The development of this institution depends largely on the real scope of decision-making on the enterprise level, on the enterprise's having its own funds to dispose of, etc. This was unequivocally proved by many research projects conducted in this field in Poland.

More complicated problems arise when one is trying to discover the impact of decentralization, as defined above, i.e., with regard to a given group of decisions only, on the direction of development of the national economy as a whole, decided on the central level. Direct interdependency is, in the author's opinion, hardly to be expected here. The question of the democratic nature of the centrally taken decisions depends more on political than on purely economic organization. Nevertheless, it would be wrong to deny any impact of the decentralization of the second group of decisions on central decisions. Autonomous activity of the lower echelons, even in the framework of general rules centrally established, creates for the central planner a certain test of independent gauges which may induce him to adapt his own decisions to the preferences expressed from below, at least in the area which does not affect the basic national preferences.

Hence, it seems possible to state that, apart from purely economic standards of efficiency, many socio-political factors also indicate the desirability of a certain degree of decentralization in a planned economy. A progressive form of social organization should contribute to overcoming alienation, to facilitating the drawing of the broad masses into active participation in shaping the development of the society, and to facilitating the manifestation of the creative ability of the members of the society. From this point of view decentralization presents undoubtedly important advantages.

## Conditions for decentralization and wider use of market mechanism

In order to make use of the merits of decentralization without impairing the foundations of a planned economy, certain important requirements have to be satisfied. They can be reduced to two points.

1. Decentralization of the second group of decisions is incompatible with an overstrained economy, unable to maintain general market equilibrium. The use of the regulated market mechanism as a means of steering the planned economy (decentralized model) is not fully possible in a situation displaying clear seller's market phenomena. It is then necessary to resort to physical allocation of resources to prevent monopolistic behaviour of the enterprises by means of administrative restrictions, etc. The difficulty of attaining conditions of more or less well-balanced growth are to a considerable extent responsible for the slow progress of decentralization in Poland during the last period.

2. The decentralization of the second group of decisions requires very precise methods of determination and correction of the operational parameters for the lower echelons, e.g., prices, wages, rates of interest, etc. These parameters must present to the enterprises the alternatives of choice in such a way as to conform to the national scale of preferences. This requires appropriate techniques for the 'translation' of physical proportions into monetary terms, e.g., the translation of the desirable structure of output into the language of price relations.

Here we face a very interesting problem of the future trends with regard to centralization and decentralization in the light of the development of new techniques of management. It is predominantly accepted that the development of modern information techniques and programming clears away the difficulties of strictly centralized management and thus makes less improbable the fulfilment of the premisses discussed in connection with our centralistic model. At the same time, however, there is good reason to assume that the development of modern information techniques will also substantially facilitate the fulfilment of the said requirements essential for decentralization in a planned economy. We have here in mind both the technical basis for planning well-balanced general proportions on the top and, what is perhaps most important, the possibility of constructing proper and sufficiently flexible sets of parameters enabling the guidance of decentralized operations in line with the interests of the national economy as a whole.

Hence, the author does not share the opinion that the progress of techniques will by itself foreclose the direction of development. The range of effective choice between centralized and decentralized organizations has to be decided from a much broader point of view, taking into account improving technical conditions in both directions.

## Reservations about the dichotomy of the two models approach

Theoretical analyses of the problems of functioning of the socialist economy in terms of the two models, centralistic and decentralized, described above are relatively widespread in the present Polish economic literature. However, attention is drawn to the danger of a rigidly dichotomous approach connected with the classification of the two models. The criticisms of a rigidly dichotomical approach were at first based mainly on purely pragmatic arguments. Lately, however, they were supported also from the theoretical side. The theoretical argumentation[5] refers to well-known critical analysis of the neo-classical assumptions about the character and shape of production function. Under the assumption of non-linear production functions, with each effective plan a system of prices can be associated which enables each economic unit, i.e., a profit maximizing enterprise, to make a rational choice consistent with the criterion of social rationality. The same set of prices could then also be used as an instrument to co-ordinate decisions in the sense of equilibrating supply and demand for factors and products. In those cases, however, when the assumption of non-linear production function cannot be upheld and one has to assume linear production functions, the use of prices, in the broad sense, as the only parameters of decisions for lower units becomes insufficient or even completely insignificant. In such cases the profit maximization would not be a sufficient criterion of choice because some irrational solutions, from the point of view of social rationality, would bring about profits equal to those resulting from the rational solutions. The informative and co-ordinative functions of prices are the more limited the higher the shares of particular suppliers of purchasers in total output of, or total demand for, the

[5] See particularly the article by J. Lipiński: 'Informacyjna funkcja cen' ('The informational function of prices'), *Ekonomista*, no. 2, 1964.

given product. This leads to the need for supplementing prices with, or even substituting for them, some quantitative non-price information. In some cases it would be sufficient to have this information generated in the process of market relations, e.g., a given demand from the product users; in some cases, however, it is argued that the necessary information has to come from higher echelons in the form of direct orders with regard to the structure of output and/or input, capital-intensity of investment, total amount of production within a given period, etc.

From the practical side the arguments against dichotomy (*either* centralization *or* decentralization of the second group of decisions) emphasize different conditions existing in different branches of the economy and difficulties in simultaneous attainment of all the necessary conditions mentioned above for a successful transition from a system based on the centralized model to the one based on the model of planned economy with a built-in market mechanism.

There is no doubt that the said reservations, both theoretical as well as practical, have to be considered to some extent. They corroborate the statement made repeatedly here that there is no practical possibility of pure model solutions. They show also the necessity of somewhat gradual transition from the centralistic institutional framework to the decentralized one.

On the other hand, however, it is also clear that every system of functioning of the economy has its internal logic which must not be impaired in essential points. An eclectic mixture of different elements from different models may often bring results worse than those which could be expected from a generally less efficient but consistently applied system. Therefore, this writer's opinion is that the system of functioning of the economy should in principle be based in a given period on very definite model-assumptions; at the same time, it should be flexible enough to permit some necessary, and temporary, departures which will prevent the system from harmful schematism. With regard to the present Polish conditions, it is the author's conviction that both the needs and the possibilities speak for essential changes towards decentralization of the second group of decisions and the broadening of the scope of application of the regulated market mechanism.

This direction of development is to some extent stated in the resolutions of the IV Congress of the Polish United Workers' Party in June 1964. The respective chapter of the resolution devoted to economic matters stresses the importance of improvement in the techniques of planning on the central level and at the same time formulates a whole series of necessary steps in the sphere of functioning of the economy. One could list the following points:[6]

. . . the enhancement of the part played by so-called synthetical success indicators (profitability, costs of production),

. . . the curtailment of the number of direct physical targets in the process of developing adequate economic instruments,

. . . the enhancement of the role of economic incentives,

. . . the perfection of the price system and the creation of conditions for a greater flexibility of prices,

. . . the transformation of the so-called industrial associations from predominantly administrative into economic units with wider possibilities of decision-making (and with simultaneous curtailment of the operative functions of the industrial ministries),

. . . the increase of the role of workers' self-management in solving problems inside the enterprise.

Similar tendencies, with lesser or greater intensity, appear in other European socialist countries. One has to keep in mind the whole complexity of the matter and thus possible discrepancies between postulates and reality; still the said tendency can be undoubtedly considered as an important confirmation of the objective character of the changes in the institutional structure of functioning of the socialist planned economy. It has to be stressed once more that we face here questions concerning changes within the framework of a centrally planned economy.

Our discussion was, for obvious reasons, limited to socialist economy. The problem of centralization and decentralization in economic management has, however, a much wider scope, with many implications for the general trends of development.

It seems that in a modern society the number of problems which

[6] See the monthly review *Nowe Drogi*, no. 7, 1964, pp. 181–4.

cannot be left to the interplay of individual interests and possibilities is steadily growing. The efforts of opponents of planning, programming, 'big government', etc., may to some extent hamper or delay certain processes, but they cannot reverse the general trend. Hence, the importance of the problem in question on a scale broader than the socialist planned economy alone.

Socialism creates, so far, the fullest conditions for the progressive tendency towards solving main socio-economic problems from the point of view of society as a whole and for consciously steering the process of development. This progressive tendency must not, however, cross the necessary boundaries and ought to leave enough room for those sources of initiative and creativity which are connected with decentralization. Hence the search for solutions, some of which were discussed here. It is to be hoped that these or similar concepts could contribute to the attainment of the necessary balance between centralization and decentralization in a planned economy.

[First published in *Hamburger Jahrbuch für Wirtschafts und Gesellschaftspolitik*, 1965.]

# 2 | Economic incentives, technical progress and the evolution of the socialist economic system

1. For the purposes of this chapter, an exact definition of technical progress is not of fundamental importance. Our subject is the economic conditions which foster or hinder innovation in the widest sense of the word. We are therefore concerned not only with the introduction of new technology and new products but also with the adaptability of producers to technical change. This does not mean that adaptability to technical progress in the strict sense, is uniform, neither does it imply a constant rate of substitution of capital for labour in processes where changes consist of increased capital intensity.

Because this article is chiefly based on the experiences of Poland (a country which, in size and in its level of development, cannot claim to be a pioneer in technical progress), it must be remembered that the problem of new techniques and new products is largely a question of adapting to our conditions those technologies already known elsewhere. This does not reduce the importance of creating and handling the appropriate economic incentives.

2. The question of incentives for technical progress in a socialist economy should first of all be considered in the light of the incentives for adaptability to technical change of the economy as a whole. It seems obvious that a planned socialist economy provides basic preconditions much more favourable to technological progress than those afforded by a capitalist economy. This may be demonstrated by the following:

a. The general purpose of economic activity in socialism (the satisfaction of social needs) means that great importance is attached to the employment of the most effective methods of production and to output. There is no parallel to the monopoly capitalist practice of resisting technological change designed to improve the use-value (i.e., the durability) of consumer goods.

b. By making economic calculations in terms of the economy as a whole, it is possible (at least in principle) to eliminate conflicts between internal and external economies. Because the total effective demand can be controlled, growth depends only on the extent and effectiveness of the resources available.

c. A planned socialist economy operates on a very wide time scale, and it is therefore possible also to consider those new production processes which bring returns only in the long run.

d. The social ownership of the means of production fosters the wide use of new methods of production. Technical information is freely available, either directly between enterprises, or indirectly through the appropriate institutions and organizations. The abolition of secrecy in production and trade is an important factor in the widespread adoption of innovations.

e. It is possible to plan the development of science and technical progress. This enables efforts to be concentrated in chosen areas. There is a danger that the importance of other areas may not be sufficiently appreciated and the spontaneity indispensable in scientific development may be weakened; but by preserving a balanced approach (an appropriate division of funds and personnel between theoretical and applied studies, between basic research and development) the advantages of planning scientific and technical progress may be obtained with the minimum of harmful effects.

f. Under capitalism, the effect of private ownership is to create a tendency to calculate the effectiveness of education by considering only the commercial advantages which accrue directly to individual enterprises. (This is also true of (e).) Socialism can take a wider view. The social aims of a socialist system include the universal availability of education; the effect of this on technical progress is obvious.

All this shows that, from the point of view of the economy as a whole, competition does not necessarily have to be the motor of technical progress. In a planned economy, leaving external factors on one side, competition, which makes innovation the condition of survival (even fictitious progress will do, provided that it has commercial effects) is replaced by the positive incentive of realizing the aims of economic operation. The pressure of competition is felt in economic relations with foreign countries—but for a country whose technical and organizational achievements fall far short of those found in more advanced economies, such competition may be useful.

The 'social monopoly', if one applies this term to a socialist economy, does not have the harmful effects on technical innovation which are produced by private monopoly. It is sometimes said that social monopoly hinders the introduction of new consumer goods; this cannot be accepted as true *a priori* because the failure to introduce such goods may be due not to the lack of incentives but to a conscious choice (e.g., in favour of capital accumulation), since the production of these new consumer goods might adversely affect the investment outlays or the balance of payments, both of which, in a rapidly developing economy, tend to be strained.

It is true that planning techniques have a conservative bias because new techniques and products are associated with increased uncertainty, but this is not a crucial factor.

In general, from a macro-economic point of view, a socialist economy tends fully to exploit technical progress. Wherever the general interests of the economy are directly felt there is no disincentive to technical advance. This is especially true of *basic investments* financed centrally. Experience shows that when new projects or general modernization are undertaken there is a tendency to choose the most advanced techniques. It is not the weakness of incentives which may affect this tendency but the availability of information, the skill of the available labour force, the extent of resources available, etc. The danger lies rather in the opposite direction, in a technocratic fascination with technical progress (this may lead to losses if some inadequately tested technique is adopted), and there may be insufficient study of the available economic alternatives. The economically optimal solution is not always that which employs the most advanced technique. Advanced methods of calculating the economic efficiency of alternative investment projects make it theoretically possible to choose the economically optimum technique. These methods are not always, however, properly employed, especially when one is trying to achieve a truly unbiased evaluation of alternative projects.

3. The problem of economic incentives for technical progress is, however, very pressing at the lower levels of the economy. (We have

not used the expression 'executive level' since this is a question which affects not only the execution of the plan but also the way in which the plan itself is drawn up.) At this level, economic incentives are designed to foster improvements in the production processes currently employed (as well as in the introduction of new products) and in the way in which the investments (on a smaller scale) are carried out by the enterprise itself. It is obvious that the extent to which technical progress is fostered in the enterprise is of great importance to the problem of technical progress as a whole, since the technical level of output, which itself constitutes the means of production, directly affects the possibilities of introducing technical progress through centrally planned investment (apart from importing machines and equipment). It is not surprising, therefore, that the central authority should exert strong pressure on the lower levels in order to ensure the fullest possible exploitation of technical progress in production methods and especially in improving the quality of goods produced. This pressure is also exercised through special sections of the plan devoted to technical progress and, even more important, through the sections dealing with production and economic targets, where the normative technical coefficients of production anticipate the introduction of new methods of production and products.

Is this pressure effective? The heart of the matter lies in the answer to this question.

The effectiveness of pressure brought to bear by the central plan on the lower levels depends, to a large extent, on how far it is possible to reconcile the general social interest with the interests of the various separate economic units and with the interests of individuals (workers, households).

If it is assumed that there are no autonomous (separate) interests and that the general social interest may be taken as being identical with that of any economic unit or individual, the whole problem could be reduced to one of the adequate provision of information. To some extent a feeling of the general harmony of these interests really does exist—apart from professional ambition, etc.—and it constitutes a direct incentive to technical progress. However, for obvious reasons, to rely on the identification of individual with social interests does not suffice; therefore, a direct connection must be established between the efforts of a given undertaking or individual with the results achieved by society. Because of this, every planned socialist economy (regardless of the extent to which it is decentralized) must assess the relative worth of these inputs and establish an appropriate set of moral and material incentives. From this follow a number of consequences which we shall consider, moving gradually, as has the economy itself, from the more to the less centralized systems.

4. In a centralized model (where the plan has the force of a command at all levels, and consumer goods and the labour force are allocated through non-market mechanisms), the central authority attempts to secure the full exploitation of technical progress by:

. . . direct technical coefficients,

. . . a directive plan of technical progress (the so-called plan of techno-organizational innovations),

. . . directives contained in the plan of the product-mix (in order to ensure the production of new or improved goods).

These methods may be very effective provided that the central authority has at its disposal:

a. independent sources of information for drawing up the plan;

b. means of ensuring that the plan is carried out (especially efficient means of quantitative and qualitative control).

These conditions can be met only in a small number of high priority projects. In the majority of cases the central authority must rely on information passed to it from below; this information may be biased by the application of the enterprises' target success indicators.

Assessments based on the fulfilment of planned tasks lead to understandable and often described pressure at the lower levels for directives which are more leisurely and therefore easier to carry out. It is difficult to overcome this tendency, even with reference to output indices (which involve a repetitive accounting of some elements), and it is still more difficult with regard to planned technological progress. Hence the higher probability of abnormal target plans in this sector: on the one hand there is a tendency to underestimate the real possibilities of the enterprises and, on the other, an inclination to introduce plans which are too rigid (as when the central planners' adjustment goes too far).

This brings us to another problem. The criteria of success, especially for enterprises, based on comparing their performances with the planned indices, are more realistic in the short term than over a longer period. This is why operational plans outweigh long-term development plans in a highly centralized economic system. This often leads to a conflict between the long time horizon necessary for assessing the effects of technological progress and the unexpectedly short time scale of the enterprise. This can be seen not only in the motivation of the enterprise managers but also in the attitude of the workers:

a. because their interests are to some extent affected by the success of the enterprise as a whole (depending on the scale of success indicators adopted by the central authority);

b. because they are concerned to maintain the existing norms, rates, etc., adopted in the calculation of their basic pay.

The more the conservative element of a system of assessment based on plan indices is strengthened, the greater is the dependence of the central authority on information provided by the lower levels. This makes it probable that the central directives will overlook the possibilities of technical progress afforded by individual improvements, in themselves comparatively small, which together might provide an important factor in development.

On the other hand when initiative comes from below (inspired by motives of material gain or by identifying personal with social interest), a highly centralized system may fail to provide the means necessary for carrying out the innovations in question. If an enterprise does not dispose of the necessary funds (with assured access to the relevant physical inputs), the implementation of technical innovations suggested from below may involve burdensome negotiations before they are accepted by the central authority. Only when the central authority has been convinced of the value of the idea will it be included in the plan and the enterprise enabled to put it into practice.

Finally, a system of success indicators, based on the comparison of performance with the plan indices when operational plans dominate, may prevent an enterprise from devoting part of its effort and resources to technical progress out of a fear that any improvements will be 'consumed' by the next plan which will simply raise its targets.

This is why enterprises press so strongly for centrally financed investment (i.e., for investment which is not a charge on the enterprise).

One of the ways of countering this is to set up at some intermediate level of the economic pyramid separate *technical progress funds* for the financing of projects with a long gestation period, losses resulting from unsuccessful projects undertaken as a calculated risk, etc. The technical progress fund is certainly useful; still its role is limited because:

. . . it is set up independently of the economic results of the enterprises and can only be drawn upon after the approval of the appropriate authorities;

. . . while it can be used to cover the costs or losses which result from the introduction of an innovation, it cannot be used to finance an enterprise's costs or losses arising from the difficulties involved in fulfilling the current plan. But it is precisely the latter phenomenon, as we have shown above, which is one of the most important disincentives to technical progress at the lower levels of the economy.

All this does not mean, of course, that those elements in the central plan designed to ensure the greatest possible use of technical advance in enterprises, branches, etc., are generally ineffective. Experience shows this not to be the case. But it is true that in this respect the plan's effectiveness is limited by factors stemming from the presumptions on which the centralized model of a planned economy is based. Hence, uneven technical progress is very characteristic of a certain stage of development in socialist countries; great advances are made in priority sectors while others remain far behind. As higher stages of development are reached, the solution of these difficulties becomes more urgent. Recently, there has been a great deal of discussion, as yet inconclusive, in which it has been suggested that the answer to this problem is to be found in decentralization and the use of a regulated market mechanism.

5. This chapter assumes that the basic outline of the arguments advanced in Poland and other socialist countries are sufficiently well known so that concepts like 'decentralization', 'regulated market mechanism', etc., may be used without causing serious misunderstanding. In particular, it must be clear that decentralization does

not mean the abandonment of central planning but represents an attempt to achieve the aims of central planning by employing what, in the opinion of many economists, is a more effective institutional structure (decentralization within a framework defined by centrally taken macro-economic decisions). The same is true of the market mechanism, which must be understood not as being opposed to the plan but as being an instrument of its fulfilment.

Decentralization and the use of a regulated market mechanism should increase the effectiveness of incentives to innovation in enterprises, branches, etc., by:

. . . increasing the importance of financial indices (profitability). This should cause enterprises to attach more importance to reducing costs and increasing sales than they do at present. It should also, by diminishing the importance of commands expressed in physical terms, encourage substitution in the factors of production, create greater elasticity in adapting the composition of output to changes in demand, etc.;

. . . tying the bonus system (including the participation of employees in profits through the 'enterprise fund') not to the plan indices, but to actual improvements in the rate of growth or the achievement of targets expressed in absolute terms;

. . . relating the size of the funds available for expansion and self-investment to financial indices. This arrangement already exists embryonically in the 'development' and 'reserve' funds, but it should be developed to the point at which, alongside the incentive to increase personal income, it acts as an incentive for those concerned to see the growth of their organization;

. . . including centrally provided investment funds in the profitability calculations (i.e., by increasing use of credit, rates of interest, etc.) made by the enterprise, so encouraging increased efficiency by the better deployment of the enterprise's own resources.

These improvements in the effectiveness of incentives for technical innovation by decentralizing the economy and the more extensive use of the market mechanism may also, however, have a number of adverse effects. There are two sets of problems here:

a. the restriction (and sometimes even the elimination) of the command system of indices for production, productivity, costs, etc., may mean a weakening of pressure exerted from above in favour of improvements in the production methods and the quality of output. At the same time there may be a failure to replace this pressure with a sufficiently long-term incentive on the part of enterprises for innovation. The time horizon of the enterprise may continue to be insufficiently wide to outweigh the short-term interests of the employees and management;

b. transferring the control of some social resources to a lower economic level may lead to a dissipation of effort and to an underestimation of the preferences of society as a whole.

Both these groups of problems are vital, even when it is assumed, as must necessarily be the case, that basic investment, especially that devoted to new projects or complete modernization, will be allocated by the central authority.

The following suggested institutional changes offer ways of counteracting these tendencies:

a. the introduction of norms binding for not less than a few years. This will help to stabilize the operating conditions and eliminate or largely reduce the fear that efforts directed to long-term ends will not be recognized;

b. the transfer of some of the responsibilities of the enterprise to the industrial association and the transformation of industrial association from an administrative unit into an economic organization (socialist corporation, trust). This would widen the time horizon (fuller study of requirements, leading to the introduction of a long-term policy with respect to techniques employed) and a better concentration of resources than if the extension of autonomy were to affect only the enterprises.

Obviously, institutional changes of this kind could only take place if the appropriate alterations were made in the external conditions under which the enterprises and industrial association operate. This would mean the active and comprehensive use of indirect instruments for influencing decisions at the lower levels in the economy by the use of a suitable price policy, tax and credit policies, etc. It is of fundamental importance that the necessary degree of price flexibility should be reconciled with the parametric role of prices for the enterprises and industrial associations, in order to prevent quasi-monopolistic behaviour. Apart from institutional changes there is also a need to put an end to the 'sellers' markets' which still abound, and thus to increase the effect of the market on the producer.

The problem described in the title of this chapter has only been sketched out here. One thing is certain, the problem which Poland, and perhaps other socialist countries, must face is not the *creation* of incentives for technical progress. What is needed is *to tap the springs of initiative in the lower levels of the economy which have not hitherto been properly exploited* while still taking full advantage of the stimuli for technical progress afforded by a socialized economy and central planning. One cannot expect an ideal solution, but the suggestions made here are offered both as envisaging more immediate economic effects and as a long-term factor in the development of the feeling that social and personal interests are intertwined in the precondition of a mature socialist society.

[First published in *Co-existence*, no. 5, Pergamon Press, 1966.]

# 3 || Economic reforms and their socio-political aspect

In the mid-1960s almost all the Eastern European socialist countries started implementing important reforms in their economic systems.

The timing, particular forms and extent of these changes differed from country to country. None the less, these reforms, if we except Yugoslavia, which needs separate consideration, were very similar in timing and in their general tendency. The general tendency was to replace a centralized system by a decentralized one, that is, to set up a planned economy employing a regulated market mechanism. 'The regulated market mechanism' is designed to replace the system of administrative directives as the link between the lower levels and the national economic plan, given that the framework within which enterprises and branches operate is defined by basic macro-economic decisions, especially those affecting investment, taken at the centre. These changes are intended to create more favourable conditions for (a) adapting the structure of supply to that of demand and eliminating the unwanted 'production for the sake of production' (b) increasing incentives for economizing production outlays, especially inputs of raw materials, which in many socialist countries are the chief constraint on growth and (c) encouraging innovation in methods of production and in introducing new products.

The similarity of the reforms in different socialist countries should be emphasized because it is a recent development. In 1956–7, when a similar and elaborate set of reforms was proposed in Poland, opinions were sharply divergent but in most socialist countries a critical attitude prevailed. It took quite a long time for it to be generally realized that the principles of a socialist planned economy cannot be laid down once and for all but, on the contrary, must be permitted to evolve, since socialism is itself subject to the general law of dialectical development. This is especially important for the adaptation of its production relations to the expansion of its productive forces in the broadest meaning of that term. Moreover, it is still expected that where demands have not been theoretically rejected, energetic and comprehensive efforts should be made to put them into operation.

Both the very need for reform and the slow rate at which reforms are introduced are often explained within the context that socialist countries are in a process of transition from an extensive to an intensive stage in their development. There is a great deal of truth in such an explanation. But it cannot automatically be accepted as the explanation of the changes in the way in which socialist economies function. For it would follow that any system of planning and management was 'right for its time', even though it had been applied to countries with different economic structures and at different levels of development. Today it is clear that at least some of the elements of the centralized system (as, for example, the practice of taking the index of gross output as the basic success indicator of an enterprise) are the cause of waste which cannot be justified at any stage of development.

The explanation of the speed with which reforms have been introduced in the course of the last decade lies in a whole series of circumstances far beyond the formula that the socialist economies are in transition from an extensive to an intensive stage in their development.

In the immediate post-Stalin period there was growing criticism of various shortcomings in economic management. But these criticisms were not always accompanied by a criticism of the centralized model as such, nor were there any fundamental criticisms of the assumptions on which the economic policy of the preceding period had been based. Doctrinal reasons account for some of this, as well as factors best described in terms of political sociology (fear of endangering the position of the existing political apparatus). Apart from these factors, however, there were a number of economic developments which, with a certain amount of wishful thinking, it was possible to adduce in support of the view that the planning and management system needed no fundamental change. First, the policy and the whole nature of the system in the last years of Stalin had so powerfully inhibited the rational exploitation of economic potential, especially in the production of consumer goods and above all in agricultural output, that all that was needed was the correction of the most obvious faults in the system in order to achieve fairly major improvements. Second, a number of investment projects were put into operation after long delays in their construction. These projects were extremely expensive but the cost of the investment involved had been basically incurred in the past. Consequently, the full force of the institutional factors impeding development was thus not immediately obvious.

The years 1956–60 (and especially the period 1956 to 1959) saw a rapid rate of growth in almost all socialist countries, hardly less in terms of general indices (the rate of growth of the national income) than the growth rate in the years immediately before 1956, while the increase in consumption was in fact much more favourable. It was these developments which made it possible to deny the need for, and to delay fundamental changes in, the economic system. There were even some instances of a return to the old indicators and methods of planning and management.

During the last phase of the period 1956–60 there were already a number of indications that 'the exploitation of earlier errors' could not last much longer. This became even more obvious during the implementation of the plans for the years 1961–5. The successes achieved in this period should not, of course, be forgotten, but neither should the failures be overlooked. These shortcomings resulted not only in a slowing of the rate of growth of national income in almost all European socialist countries (with the exception of Rumania) but, most of all, an unexpectedly low effectiveness of investment (a number of important plan indices were unfulfilled, while the increase in investments and employment was actually greater than that provided for in the plan).

It is no accident that the sharpest declines in the rate of growth were felt in the most developed of the socialist countries. The average yearly rate of growth in Czechoslovakia for the years 1961–5 was 2 per cent as compared with 7 per cent in the preceding five years; in the German Democratic Republic, for the same periods, the rate of growth fell from 8 to 3 per cent.[1] The more complicated structure

---

[1] In Poland the fall in the rate of growth was negligible (6 per cent as against 6·6 per cent in the preceding five years). None the less here too the planned increase in national income was only achieved by exceeding the targets for

of a highly developed economy means that all those failures normally associated with a centralized model were accentuated: a lack of technical innovation in enterprises, inadequate flexibility in adapting the structure of output to demand, an inadequate appreciation of the importance of economizing in labour and material outlays, a failure to improve quality, etc. When it is remembered that in Czechoslovakia, the German Democratic Republic and Hungary there are no labour reserves which can be used to substitute extensive for intensive development and also that the economies of these countries are heavily dependent on foreign trade, it is not surprising that failure should have been so extensive or that pressure for reform should have been so great.

The rate of growth of national income has here been taken as an index of the declining efficiency of the old economic system. It is clear, however, that in the last analysis the real criteria for success should be sought in the consumer sector. In this area the failure to meet the planned targets was even greater, both in terms of current real incomes and in terms of investment in collective consumption sectors.

It would be a mistake to attribute the economic shortcomings of socialist countries exclusively to the functioning of their economic systems. For the same reason, as discussions of the subject have often emphasized, even the most careful of economic reforms cannot be expected of themselves to solve all the problems and clear away all the obstacles. Illusions on this point are dangerous.

But, even given these qualifications, I think that there is a demonstrable connection between the system of planning and management on the one hand and the efficiency with which the economy is operated on the other. The proposals for reform to which an assessment of the previous period gave rise are therefore certainly sound. The

---

investment and employment. In the USSR the average yearly growth rate in 1961–5 was something over 6 per cent as against 9 per cent in the previous five years. In the case of Poland and the USSR, as well as of Rumania and Bulgaria, because of the relatively large numbers employed in agriculture, it is still possible to get a certain amount of growth by extensive methods. Even these countries, however, are experiencing difficulties of the kind described, albeit from a purely economic point of view, less sharply and somewhat later than others.

fast and consistent implementation of these reforms is a necessary, though not sufficient, condition for the rapid and effective growth of a socialist economy.

These proposals for reform have been greeted by some as heralding the abandonment of planning: this has given satisfaction to some bourgeois economists and journalists and has been deplored in some Marxist circles. These reactions are based on the erroneous idea that plan and market are mutually exclusive economic institutions. The plan is identified with a system in which directives are enforced by orders, while the market is thought of as a spontaneously self-regulating mechanism which, by definition, precludes the social handling of economic processes.

These ideas I believe to be wrong. Socialist planning is the conscious allocation of resources in order to achieve the maximum satisfaction of social needs. It is to this end that the institutions of a planned economy must be subordinated—nor is the command system of the centralized economy the only form which such institutions may take. In some circumstances a *regulated* market mechanism is (or may at least appear to be) the form better suited to a planned economy than a command mechanism. Moreover, when the growth of a socialist economy makes its structure more complex, when the plan has to accommodate a large number of priorities, when quantitative targets can only be achieved by improving the quality and diversity of production and by technological innovation, by increasing foreign trade, etc., when the satisfaction of consumer demand—both as an aim in itself and also in order to increase productivity—calls for an appropriate elasticity in the supply arrangements—the use of the market is not only desirable but inevitable (however paradoxical that may sound!) in order to ensure the success of the plan. The maintenance of old methods of detailed direct planning of the centralized type leads not only to a fall in efficiency but may mean also that control of many of the links in the economic process is lost: the capacity of the channels of information and the ability of the centre to process the data are inadequate, so that their supply is slowed down and distortions set in (the distortions resulting from this will not cancel each other out but, because of a whole system of

35

vested interests, will build up). This is the reason why the use of some kind of self-regulating device in a planned economy is so important. Such a device is provided by a market mechanism which is only broadly controlled by the central authority. It is precisely this problem of controlling decentralized decisions that is stressed by the prominent Soviet mathematical economist, Novozhilov, in talking about the 'direct' and 'indirect' (market) centralization of economic decisions.[2]

> The direct and centralized solution of economic problems depends on the central planning authority taking concrete decisions. Indirect centralization . . . is achieved by establishing parameters for the calculation of investment, with the help of which the local authorities . . . can find variants which best correspond to the general economic plan . . . Indirect centralization is indispensable both under socialism and under communism . . . [since] it subordinates to the central plan *all* local decisions without exception right down to the most detailed.

It is clear that in order to achieve the effects which the reforms are intended to produce—the strengthening of the planning system with the assistance of the regulated market mechanism to improve the plan's consistency and effectiveness—a number of complex conditions must be fulfilled. It is of particular importance that each stage of the transition to the new system should be synchronized with the setting up of the appropriate instruments of economic control.

Because a great deal of thought had already been devoted to this problem, it was possible to include in the reforms a whole series of measures designed to resolve it. These included changes in central planning methods, in economic institutions, in the structure of prices and the way in which they were determined, and in the indices and incentives governing the rules of behaviour for enterprises. All these matters are the subject of discussion, experiment and study, and although many issues remain to be settled they are all recognized as real problems.

However, neither the substance nor the consequences of planning

[2] *Ekonomika i matematicheskie metody* (*Economics and mathematical methods*), vol. 1, no. 5, Moscow, 1965.

and institutional reforms is purely economic—and this is especially true of techno-economic, managerial changes. These are of *great social and political importance* and must therefore be considered in the context of the whole socialist transformation of society. Unfortunately, this side of the question is still quite obscure. It may therefore be useful for the purposes of illustration to consider some of its general aspects.

Let us take, for example, the question of economic incentives. At one time any tendency to increase the importance of economic incentives in a centralized system was regarded as something which it was difficult to reconcile with the long-term ideals of a socialist and integrated society where non-economic motives should dominate and actions should be dictated by idealism, a sense of solidarity, social duty, and so on. Nowadays this tendency appears to be the subject of fewer doubts in European socialist countries (although it still gives cause for excitement in various left-wing circles in the West). But economic reform does not consist so much in the introduction of economic incentives but rather in an alteration in their nature. The way to increase the effectiveness of incentives is to ensure that they provide a proper link between individual and social interests. If this is done, or even if something close to this can be achieved, then the factors fostering integration, coupled with political education in the socialist ideals of communal life, will operate more powerfully than in the present situation, where in many ways the system of incentives is an expression of the antagonisms between the social interests and those of individuals, not of their harmony.

There are, connected with this general problem, other issues, which have not been adequately studied in the socio-economic literature of socialist countries—in some areas there are complete blanks. The most glaring omission is the existence of any discussion of the effect which changes in the system of economic planning and management may have on the *social structure of incomes*, on income differentiation.

It is sometimes believed that an increase in the effectiveness of economic incentives inevitably produces a greater differentiation between the earnings of different groups of workers and, in particular, raises the incomes of managerial personnel. But, in theory at least, there is not and ought not to be a direct and simple relationship between the development of economic decentralization and an increased disparity in individual incomes. It follows from what we have already said that the main element in the reforms is a change in the system of incentives, that is, an alteration in the way in which these are related to the results achieved, with more attention being given to the contribution of particular individuals and groups in the distribution of funds, etc. This does not automatically involve an increase in the disparity of incomes, especially if we suppose that the social factor plays a greater part (especially in the form of workers' self-government) in determining income structure. Planning and management reform will of itself cause certain changes in income structure but these will be of different kinds (in some cases greater disparity in incomes, in other cases, less). These changes will result from a reassessment of the relative importance to the economy of various kinds of employment. There is (and this also ought to be considered) the serious question of differences in income as between different groups of workers which will be caused by the greater use of synthetic financial indices, but this is a different kind of problem.

If it would be wrong, therefore, to suppose that economic reforms themselves determine changes in income structure, then this question is one which still remains open to the general economic policy. The conflict between the need to preserve a difference in incomes on the one hand and socialist egalitarianism on the other is one of those fundamental contradictions in socialism which cannot be resolved at a stroke. None the less, the political and economic programmes should perhaps acknowledge more openly than they have done so far that this conflict does exist. This will help to keep the disparities in income, which are a necessary accompaniment to the present stage in our development, within limits and to minimize their effects.

More attention should be paid to this problem in the preparation of plans and in the economic analysis of the situation. Apart from the general observation that income is more evenly distributed than under capitalism the scanty and vague information which we possess enables us to say very little about the present state of or trends in the social distribution of income.

The harmful effects of the uneven distribution of income are felt more strongly now than immediately after the institution of socialism, because the period following the revolution was one of great social mobility, and there were greater possibilities of massive social advance. The stabilization which followed tended to perpetuate to a certain extent the differences between the rungs of the social hierarchy along with the differences in income. This threatened to petrify the stratification of society by penalizing children for the lower incomes of their parents (inequality of opportunity).

This brings us to the next problem which is often associated with economic reforms. This is the problem of *social services rendered from the collective consumption fund* (including investment in projects from which the direct services to the public are rendered), their long-term development, rate of growth, relationship to private consumption, etc. Obviously, services rendered from the collective consumption fund, apart from a number of other functions, play an important role in evening out disparities in incomes and particularly in minimizing the effect of these disparities on opportunities available to young people.

It is believed that economic reforms should provide that as the principle of profitability is introduced there should be a correspondingly wider use of payments for social services. Evidence that this has in fact occurred in recent years can be found in a number of countries, especially in their housing sectors, and this is supposed to prove the case.

Although individual decisions must be considered in the context of time and place, it would, I think, be wrong to assert that the demand for payment in return for a number of social services hitherto provided free is always rooted in a system of incentives. Economic reforms are designed to increase the effectiveness of economic outlays, but are not an end in themselves. There is no reason why they should impede the achievement of socialism's long-term goals, among which equality—at least in the sense of equality of opportunity—occupies one of the chief places. In the long term, equality is economically as well as socially, important, since it makes it possible to exploit the full potential of human abilities.

There is, of course, a conflict between the respective shares of collective and individual consumption in the national income, a conflict whose intensity varies inversely with the size of the funds available for total consumption and with the average level of individual incomes. The resolution of this conflict depends, in every case, on many circumstances. The need for pragmatism in planning should not, however, hinder the application of the basic criteria. In the case we have been discussing the criteria are not yet clear and need to be systematically studied. One thing is clear: the need to increase the part played by incentives in determining the behaviour of individual units engaged in economic activities is not a principle which can be automatically applied on the level of collective consumption which is one of the significant elements in the distribution of the national income under socialism.

The general outline of the problems set out above cannot be used to draw conclusions of direct significance for economic policy. No quantitative suggestions are offered either in respect of the development of incomes or of the proper division of funds between collective and individual consumption. I wish only to make one general point—and that is that the improvement of the planning and economic system cannot be confined to institutional changes but must also ensure that the central planner takes greater account of social problems.

In our planning documents there is a great deal of information about the changes which are to take place in output and the average consumption of goods, the size of the necessary investments, etc. There is, on the other hand, no description of changes in the social structure, no explanation of the direction of change and no account of the means to be used to ensure that changes are of the kind desired. Increasing the scope of the plan will meet with great technical and conceptual difficulties. It seems likely, however, that the need for such an extension becomes more acute, in part as a result of the reform of the economic system in its strict sense; first, because a decentralized model attaches greater importance to long-term plans and these, in the nature of things, must take greater account of socio-economic problems; second, because an increase in the autonomy and significance of the market mechanism for the operations of enterprises increases the responsibility of the central planner in precisely defining the general directions of development.

The social problem of reform is not confined, however, to the *content* of the new economic policy. There is also the question of the socio-political aspect of the economic *mechanism* employed in a decentralized economy and the socio-political problems connected with carrying out the reforms themselves. Both these problems are closely connected with each other.

The first problem includes the complex of issues connected with workers' participation in the management of a socialized economy. At the enterprise level this participation takes the form of the workers' council, the idea and realization of which are an inseparable part of the move towards decentralization. This is demonstrated by the practice of a number of socialist countries: economic reforms go hand in hand with the creation of workers' councils, although the names, powers and, especially, real significance of these institutions varies. It is hard to believe that this is accidental. The participation of the workers in management is an indispensable part of a system in which central planning is combined with a given degree of autonomy for enterprises. The purpose of this autonomy is to release the initiative of those directly engaged in the production process and this can only be exploited by creating a feeling of responsibility for the success of the enterprise as a whole which, in turn, cannot be expected unless employees have a real influence on the running of their enterprise. Real workers' participation in management is especially important in widening the time horizon of the enterprise's operations. One of the most serious failings of the present economic system is the sharp contradiction between the wide time horizon of the central plan and the extraordinarily narrow time horizon of the enterprises. In attempts to meet their targets (fixed by the central plan), the enterprises often use less economic methods which, however, allow them to achieve results within the period of the plan. There is no need to stress how this hampers technical progress in the existing enterprises and retards their adaptation to changes in the structure of demand, etc. The resolution of this contradiction requires not only that the central interest should be shifted from the short- to the medium- and long-term plans but also that an investor may expect to benefit from risk-taking in investment. An enterprise must be able to work for its long-term interests and the best way of ensuring this is to develop collective decision-making, collective incentives and collective responsibility.

This is a complex problem and it would be hard to expect it to be resolved by the changes sketched out here. Labour turnover makes it difficult to involve the employees in the long-term goals of an enterprise. However, as against this, in the first place, let us note that changes in personnel take place gradually (so preserving continuity) and that, in the second place, the development of workers' councils and the setting up of long-term economic incentives may themselves reduce labour turnover. It is thus the case that—although we are dealing here with the question of the whole development of socialist relations—consistent and thorough reform combined with the strengthening of workers' councils may help to improve the situation.

There are many reasons why we are still a long way from full employee participation in management. One of the more important of these reasons is the fear of disturbing any of the elements in the existing political structure; as a result, workers' councils are submerged in the existing institutional framework, dominated by the party and trade union apparatus which is itself directly controlled by the upper levels of the hierarchy. This state of affairs is largely due to the maintenance of the overcentralized economic system which, by cramping the enterprise, fails to provide a proper area of competence for the workers' council. There is, moreover, a tendency on the part of management to underestimate the importance of workers' councils and a reluctance on the part of managerial personnel 'to share power'. The participation of workers in management is sometimes regarded as a formal concession to ideology, the real implementation of which would only reduce efficiency. The defeat of these short-sighted ideas is one of the fundamental conditions for the success of the reforms.

In order that the workers' council may fulfil the task allotted to it in the new economic model, there must be a ready acceptance of participation in management by the broad masses of the workers. Such an attitude will not arise of its own accord simply in response to an announcement that workers' councils are to be instituted. A political atmosphere in which a feeling for the need and value of participation in general affairs is engendered, and positive experience of the effectiveness of such an attitude is provided, is absolutely vital.

It is not easy to judge how far these preconditions exist or are developing in the various countries in which reforms have been introduced. In Poland much remains to be done; indeed, much remains to be done in order to catch up. In 1956 a powerful and spontaneous mass movement set up workers' councils in many industrial centres. The idea of workers' co-management was bound up with a whole programme of political and economic change. Today it would be difficult to claim that there is any such mass interest in the reform of the system, that any great hopes are placed in it, or that there is any enthusiasm for the idea of workers' self-government.

This raises another important problem—the part played by changes in the economic system in the general development of socialist society. Increased independence for enterprises or local authorities, together with reforms of the kind we have discussed, are of great importance because they create, as we have stressed, the preconditions for the development of workers' self-government at the lower levels of the economy. While fully appreciating the desirability of this kind of change it must be remembered that this is not *of itself* sufficient to ensure the rate of growth and the scale of progress necessary for the evolution of socialist relations of production. In a planned economy the situation in a given factory or region must depend on the situation in the economy as a whole, that is, on macro-economic decisions. It is wrong to confine the democratization of the management of the nationalized means of production to the enterprise or the region; moreover, such a restriction may, in the long run, *intensify* the conflict between the interests of particular groups and the interests of society as a whole.

In order that the decentralized system shall be effective, both economically and socio-politically, society must be enabled to exercise a real influence on *those general* decisions dealing with the distribution and utilization of the national income, and especially on the formulation of the long-term economic plans and their social consequences.

Whether the arguments set out above are accepted or not, it is clear that the success of the programme of economic reforms I have outlined depends not only on techno-economic solutions but also on the degree to which attention is devoted to the socio-political aspect of the question.

[First published in *Gospodarka Planowa* (*The Planned Economy*), no. 11, Warsaw, 1966.]

# 4 | Commodity fetishism and socialism

The theory of commodity fetishism has always been regarded as a fundamental element of Marxian economic theory. It may be said to have performed two functions at connected, but different levels: substantively, in the analysis of the commodity economy and the capitalist commodity economy in particular, and methodologically, in the examination of the general relationship between the form and content of socio-economic phenomena.

A question which was once often put and which deserves consideration, perhaps especially today, runs as follows—to what extent, if at all, is the theory of commodity fetishism of significance, especially with reference to a socialist system? This essay is an attempt to answer this question although in general and tentative terms.

## I

I shall assume that the basic propositions of the theory of commodity fetishism are known and shall limit myself to the briefest possible description of them. Any description is itself, of course, to some degree an account of the author's own views, at least as far as his understanding of Marx is concerned. As far as possible I shall avoid using strictly philosophical language over which, in this area, hangs the heavy tradition of Hegelianism.

1. The theory of commodity fetishism I understand primarily as a critique of the objective situation of man in the commodity economy. The most important points of this critique are as follows:

a. the relations between men are objectified in the form of exchange relations between goods;

b. the social character of labour is obscured—on the surface the labour of the producer of commodities appears as private labour, and this finds expression in the maximization of private advantage and results in social atomization;

c. economic and social processes are the spontaneously determined resultant of the activities of isolated producers obliged to
adapt themselves to factors over which they have no control—the
general level of technological development, the movements in prices,
wages, employment, etc.

In general, the theory of commodity fetishism describes a situation
in which alienation predominates, arising from the fact that, as
Marx writes in *The German Ideology*, 'The social power . . . which
arises through the co-operation of different individuals . . . appears
to these individuals . . . not as their own united power, but as an
alien force existing outside them, of the origin and goal of which
they are ignorant, which they thus cannot control.'[1] The theory of
commodity fetishism is the foundation on which Marx constructs the
fetishism of money and the fetishism of capital.

In his critique of commodity production in general and of capitalist commodity production in particular, however, Marx never
abandons the principle of *historicism*. It is, therefore, a relativistic
critique and does not deny that in certain circumstances commodity
relations may be progressive.

2. The theory of commodity fetishism is a critique of 'false consciousness', of the ideology which arises from the capitalist commodity economy. The function of this ideology in a political economy
is that of an apologia for the market as an institution, which is supposed to guarantee the *optimal* allocation of resources, the *equality*
of participants in exchange, *freedom* of choice and the *sovereignty* of
the consumer, just *rewards* of the factors of production (in proportion
to their productivity), etc.

The whole of *Capital*—from chapter 1, where Marx explains the
theory of commodity fetishism, to the last chapter of volume III—
is a critique of this economic ideology. And again, this is a historical
critique, pointing only to the relative values of the market mechanism of allocation and so stressing their transient nature; showing
that it is wrong to treat commodity relations as some sort of 'natural'
relationship between people in the economic process.

3. The theory of commodity fetishism is a particular case of the

[1] London, 1965, p. 46.

analysis of the relationship between the form and content of social phenomena. In this sense it has a wider methodological significance as the critique of the fetishism of forms in general. The discovery of the real content of social relationships behind the forms in which they are mythologized and masked is thus the principal task of the social sciences.

## II

As we have shown, the theory of commodity fetishism in *Capital* provides a general basis for the analysis of the fetishism of capitalist relations of production. Its influence on Marxist thought was so powerful that for a long time the liberation of labour under socialism was thought of not only as its liberation from capital but also as *the complete abolition of the commodity forms of social relations.* The origin of this attitude is to be found in Marx at the very beginning of his work in the first chapter of volume I of *Capital* in the section dealing with the fetishism of commodities, where he contrasts the 'mystification of the world of commodities' with 'a community of free individuals, carrying on their work with the means of production in common, in which the labour power of all the different individuals is consciously applied as the combined labour-power of the community.'[2]

Further, from the statement: 'The social relations of the individual producers, with regard both to their labour and to its products, are in this case perfectly simple and intelligible, and that with regard not only to production but also to distribution,'[3] it was deduced that the transition from capitalism to socialism meant the end of social sciences as previously understood because the problem of laying bare the real content of social relationships, which were hidden behind their fetishized forms, would no longer be relevant. Its place would be taken—it was thought—by a kind of economic engineering—the science of the rational *organization of productive forces.*

Reality, however, proved to be less straightforward, both with regard to the appearance of commodity relations and with respect to the general problem of the fetishism of forms.

[2] Moscow, 1965, vol. 1, p. 78.
[3] *Capital*, vol. 1, p. 79.

Commodity relations in the socialist system proved to be more durable than had been expected and, what is perhaps more important, their extent and significance have increased, at least by comparison with the situation immediately after the revolution. Even if we ignore the Soviet development from war communism to NEP, taking 1929–30 as a starting point, and corresponding periods in the Peoples' Democracies, the general trend is quite clear—starting from a pretty thorough-going distribution *in natura*, development proceeds by way of the adoption of commodity relations in consumption and market forms of the allocation of the labour force to an increasing use of commodity relations between state enterprises, the more confident use of market forms of the implementation of the central plan, etc. The direction of economic reforms in almost all European socialist countries, together with an increasing tendency for certain needs, hitherto regarded as the province of social services, to be left to, and paid from, the resources of the individual—all this leaves little doubt as to the direction of change.

Of course, this does not mean that this trend has received universal approbation, though there have been some radical changes of opinion. Although there persistently came to the surface ideas rooted in a purely definitional attitude towards economic phenomena under socialism (in statements such as: 'since this is a socialist system there are no commodities' or 'there are commodities and therefore this system cannot be socialist'), this is a purely marginal phenomenon without any influence on scientific opinion, let alone on the real course of events. The primitive nature of this attitude, which attempts to substitute for an appreciation of the contradictory aspects of reality a verbal resolution of a closed circle of definitions, is all too clear.

At another level, the nature of particular commodity relations under socialism, their extent, long-term development, etc., have already been discussed. Here, an attempt is being made to 'legitimize' commodity relations under socialism, to search for real solutions and to find answers to basic questions. And here the Big Bertha of 'revisionism' is sometimes to be seen, but (a) the shells fall further and further from their target (the accusation of revisionism is turned against those who are said to advocate too wide a field for commodity relations instead of being aimed at those who insist that they exist at all) and (b) recent experience, especially in the Poland of 1968, has shown that even a violent 'anti-revisionist' storm cannot obviate the need for a discussion of economic reforms, which leads, willy-nilly, to an increase in the extent to which commodity relations are allowed to operate in a planned socialist economy. At times of political crisis pathetic attempts are sometimes made to use the bogeyman of 'market socialism' in attacks on particular individuals but, so far, this has not led to any reversal in the tendency which I have described. It may sound paradoxical, but the failure of successive anti-revisionist campaigns provides, in its own way, proof of the objective nature of the basis of commodity relations at the present stage of development in European socialist countries.

This development bears out the importance of a concrete and historical approach to the problem of commodity relations under socialism. In given socio-economic circumstances an increase in the scope and the importance of commodity relations may, for a number of reasons, greatly facilitate the development of a socialist society. Several important areas in which—as has often been stated in discussions of this subject—positive effects may be felt are as follows:

. . . an increase in the effectiveness of economic management and increased elasticity in the adaptation of production to needs;

. . . more effective central planning and control of the economic process at the macro-economic level; appearances notwithstanding, the increased use of indirect instruments of control, the so-called market mechanism, is in certain circumstances absolutely vital to the command of the whole complex of increasingly complicated economic relationships. Similarly, the universal application of direct commands may give rise to a dangerous fiction which only conceals the enormous growth of spontaneity, eroding the foundations of central planning;

. . . encouraging the *process* of integrating the goals in separate areas (individual and group) with the general goals; this is the result of the often discussed complex of problems connected with the possibilities for economic incentives opened up by the increased use of the market mechanism: if by this means the connection between individual (and collective) interests and social interests were really to be strengthened, this would not merely improve short-term economic efficiency but, most important, would have educational effects, providing a much more powerful impulse for the growth of socialist consciousness than can be derived from verbal didacticism;

. . . the next point is closely connected with the previous one. This is the question of the relationship between the scope of commodity relations and autonomous decentralized decisions on one hand, and the real preconditions for workers' self-government as the vital element in socialist democracy on the other. Clearly, it is no accident that in all economic reforms attempted so far, the postulation of the wider use of the market mechanism in a planned economy has always been accompanied by the idea of workers' self-government;

. . . all this leads one to expect that economic reform will foster the development of creative initiative, especially in the sphere of technological progress and organizational improvement.

There is no need to dwell for long on this aspect of the problem which has been discussed so often in the recent past. It is the second side of the question which is so important—is that aspect of commodity relations which Marx described as commodity fetishism quite extinct in our system? This question may be thought to be premature in a situation where, as I think, so much still remains to be done in order to carry out economic reforms to increase the scope of commodity relations as an instrument of planning. A one-sided approach could, however, have serious consequences, especially by taking us from one extreme to another, and this must be avoided at whatever cost in terms of tactics.

There are contradictions in every phenomenon at any moment. Therefore commodity relations in a socialist system cannot be free from them. Even in our own society commodity forms of human relationships are pregnant with many dangers.

In the most general terms, the development of commodity relations means the increased isolation of those engaged in economic activity and the increased autonomy of individual interests with respect to the interest of society as a whole. This can have a number of undesirable effects from the point of view of both the short- and long-term aims of a socialist system:

. . . the realization of personal interests at the cost of the social interest by a disproportionate share in income; this results from the practice of relating income to economic performance and extending the scope of commodity relations requires that this effect should be strengthened (see below); ·

. . . the antagonism between personal and social interests may be further intensified when it moves to the level of the relationships between enterprises, taken together, and society as a whole. Here, because of their size, enterprises have a greater bargaining power than individuals. Because in the real world there are no perfect markets, this means that one must reckon with the exploitation of monopolistic positions not only in order to impose excessive prices but also in order to corner the labour market, to manipulate the degree of utilization of productive capacities, etc.;

. . . the increased importance of the market and the linking of individual incomes with the economic success of enterprises mean that some consideration must be given to the effect of gambling on the market situation. On the one hand, the linking of individual wages with the economic results of enterprises should be approved of, from the point of view of the principle of distribution according to labour input. On the other, it may be necessary to compensate for failures independent of the performance of enterprises and to neutralize the effect of a feeling of instability;

. . . the granting of genuine autonomy to individual economic units of the national economy may endanger the global character of economic calculus by not allowing for inputs and outputs which are external from the point of view of the enterprise in question. It may also lead to a narrowing of its time horizon;

. . . all these (and analogous) factors may have an adverse effect on social consciousness, lead to a feeling that human relationships have been commercialized, weaken the operation of the principle of solidarity, etc.

All this would seem to indicate that even a full recognition of the necessity of increasing the scope and function of commodity relations in a given phase of the development of socialism must not be allowed to obscure the connection between this and the undesirable side-effects which may, and to a certain extent must, follow. This is true both with regard to objective situations, the position of individuals in the process of production and distribution, as well as in respect to the subjective reflection of these situations in consciousness. In this sense the Marxist theory of commodity fetishism is still valid for socialism and indeed for each of its stages of development, since (a) so far, commodity relations have always existed in some degree and (b) the principle of distribution according to labour inputs is, as Marx observed in his *Critique of the Gotha Programme,* in some respects quite similar to commodity exchange (*do ut des* in the relationship between society and the individual). This is even more relevant to situations in which the part played by commodity relations is more than minimal.

## III

The theory of commodity fetishism does not, therefore, lead to the conclusion that in socialism commodity relations and socialism are incompatible but, rather, it raises the question of the limitations within which commodity and market forms of relationship may be exploited. Playing with words a little, one might say that the theory of commodity fetishism carries a necessary warning against the fetishism of commodity-money mechanisms in a planned socialist economy.

In what does this kind of fetishism consist? The briefest and therefore the most general answer to this question is that it lies in treating the socialist economy simply as a *commodity economy,* an economy in which, moreover (and this is of fundamental importance), individual units engaged in economic activity employ socialized means of production which have been separated from the whole. I do not wish to create the impression that I attribute a mystical power to words but I do think that the expression 'the socialist economy *is* a commodity economy' as opposed, for example, to the expression 'commodity relations are to be found in a socialist economy' has important theoretical and, in certain circumstances, practical consequences.

The definition of the socialist economy as a commodity economy dismisses the whole problem of the boundaries within which commodity relations may be allowed to operate and eliminates this issue from the range of alternatives with which we are faced in the conscious social *choice* of a system for the operation of the economy. Hence, the question of choice in its instrumental sense does not arise, especially in the long run, because socialist production is, in the nature of things, commodity production, the production of *exchange* value. Each producer's objective function is thus unequivocally determined in the sense that the target of each productive unit exists separately from and independently of any overriding economic target at the national level. The adoption of a definition of the socialist economy as a commodity economy really involves the disappearance of the hierarchical structure of aims (in Lange's terms) as well as the priority accorded to the production of use-values for which the production of exchange values can only be an effective means but which cannot be a substitute.[4] The total effect is then the sum of individual effects just as total input is the sum of individual outlays. It is difficult to imagine if and how, in an economy consistently treated as a commodity economy, it is possible to take external economies and diseconomies into account, since the very idea involves the relationship of parts to the whole, of a sub-system to the system, and so implies the existence of some superior objective function along with a direct calculation of optimization in terms of it.

It is, however, clear that in a commodity economy in the strict sense, the rules of behaviour of the economic units are entirely determined by the operation of the law of value, and general equilibrium is the resultant of the striving for equilibrium by the individual units involved. The structure of prices must, as a result, be determined by this striving for equilibrium, while the question of how far the set of equilibrium prices reflects opportunity costs in the economy as a whole, does not arise, because the category of social opportunity cost (as a category distinct from market prices) has no place in a strictly defined model of a commodity economy.

Of course, one must not ignore the influence of socialist relations of production and of social ownership on the functioning of such a commodity economy. The fact that the commodity producers are

[4] See Edward Lipiński, *Teoria ekonomii i aktualne zagadnienia gospodarcze* (*Economic theory and current economic problems*), Warsaw, 1961, especially the article 'Wartość użytkowa w ekonomii socjalizmu' ('Use value in socialist economics'), first published in *Ekonomista*, no. 4, 1948.

socialist and collective is especially reflected in the objective function which cannot now be maximization of return on capital but is given by the maximization of incomes which are distributed according to labour input and determined by the economic success of the individual institution (e.g., the enterprise). Assuming that the operating unit is a workers' collective, the rules of behaviour in a socialist commodity economy will be determined, as it were, naturally, for it will not be possible to decide it from above for the sake of some overriding interest (see, e.g., Lange's model described in *On the Economic Theory of Socialism*).[5] *This natural rule of behaviour* (for purely economic purposes) will be, in a socialist commodity economy, *the maximization of net income per employee* (i.e., net of taxes, and given a system of distribution of incomes among the employees of the enterprise). There is no need to lay down this rule—the rule establishes itself, provided that it is not impeded by some external action in the general interest, an action anyway contradicting the unqualified definition of a commodity economy. It is worth remembering at this point that the rule of maximizing income per employee has a very definite effect on the point of equilibrium of an enterprise at given productive capacities (*ceteris paribus*, equilibrium will be reached at a lower level of output and employment than would prevail in an enterprise maximizing profit), and will also influence the choice of technique of production (there will be a tendency to employ more capital-intensive techniques, i.e., with a higher capital/labour ratio). Naturally, it is possible to affect the point of equilibrium of an enterprise by the appropriate instruments at the disposal of the state (especially by a prices policy and a system of taxation, in the broad sense of this term), but (a) since the objective function cannot be determined from above, the effectiveness of these instruments is limited and (b) the very employment of these instruments is at variance with the definition adopted.

In reality, if there is in reality anything which could satisfactorily correspond with our theoretical notions (the Yugoslav model which the reforms of 1965 were designed to produce perhaps comes nearest to it), especially in modern circumstances, an active economic policy

[5] Minneapolis, 1938.

cannot be eliminated. When the elements of such a policy are sufficiently closely co-ordinated, one may even be tempted to describe them as 'planning'. But if the socialist economy is consistently understood as a commodity economy, it seems that this reduces the role of planning to no more than three functions:

1. the prediction of the general trend of development;

2. the neutralizing of 'imperfections' in the market (the effectiveness of this function may prove to be limited because of the economic and technical tendency towards concentration);

3. the correction of market processes in particular cases where the market fails to respond, or operates in a way which is clearly contrary to the long-term interests of society (the development of extremely backward regions, acute social problems, etc.).

Hence, if we adopt the interpretation of a socialist commodity economy outlined above, then it is difficult to see in such a system any role for planning apart from that of providing, in certain situations, a corrective to the fundamental allocative function of the market mechanism.

## IV

Whether or not a socialist economy is a commodity economy decides whether or not there is any conscious choice of the mechanism by which the economy is to function. In rejecting the definition discussed above we discard at the same time the *absolute* character of commodity forms of economic relations—and this, in my opinion, is the very essence of commodity fetishism in economics, as opposed to the view which sees fetishism in every use of commodity relations in a socialist economy. A society which consciously constructs a mechanism for the functioning of its economy chooses between different combinations of direct and market forms of allocation, and subordinates commodity relations to autonomously defined goals and criteria of rationality. In this way, society can overcome commodity fetishism, especially those aspects of it which derive from the atomization of society, without losing the opportunity of employing commodity relations in areas where, at a given stage of development, they will assist in the attainment of social aims. The use of the market mechanism in a planned economy may of course, even so, have undesirable side-effects but (a) the use of the proper institutional arrangements should mean that the disadvantages are less than the advantages, and (b) direct measures may be taken to counter them.

The primary theoretical assumption in this approach to the problem is that socialist society is, in the last analysis, the producer of use-values, a society for which the final end is consumption and labour the measure of inputs. This means that it is both necessary and possible (although, in the light of the difficulties of programming when multiplicity of aims is involved, by no means easy) to lay down macro-economic targets and means on a social scale, especially for long-term projects. This makes it necessary to 'internalize' many factors which, in a commodity economy, *sensu stricto*, are regarded as externalities. To give a simple example—the failure to exploit labour resources (unemployment) costs the enterprise nothing, but it is a social cost and therefore ought to be included in the economic calculus.

This makes it necessary to operate in terms of social cost, calculated in a sense directly, i.e., not as a function of current market processes and the behaviour of autonomous producers. The social opportunity cost must be deduced from *a general economic programme of optimization* (a plan which should be the closest possible approximation to the optimal solution), i.e. a programme which is based on a given objective function and on the constraints on the system as a whole, within a given time horizon. The opportunity costs so arrived at should be expressed in a set of *'normal' prices* ('initial prices' in the terminology employed a few years ago—now it is more usual to speak of 'programming prices'), which in turn should be the basis for a set of market prices. The difference between this arrangement and the system described in the previous section is illustrated, for instance, by one of the few quantities derived for practical purposes from a special optimizing programme in Poland. I have in mind the recoupment period for the return on incremental investment outlays on the one hand and the market rate of interest on the other. The problem is not only, or even not so much, that of uncontrolled changes in the rate of interest—fluctuations which are becoming less and less frepuent; however, even when the interest rate is closely controlled, for instance by central financial institutions, it still has a point of equilibrium dependent on demand and supply in the capital market, and therefore ultimately on micro-economic decisions. The recoupment period, in the sense of a general economic norm of the effectiveness of investment, is, by contrast, deduced from macro-economic assumptions, including the objective function and constraints. This recoupment period is then used by individual investors in their calculations as an element in their decision-making while the scope of their decisions is obviously determined (the recoupment period is a device for selecting the technical variant of a particular investment project but is not designed for use in inter-industry comparisons of investment effectiveness; i.e., it is not designed for the determining of the future inter-industry structure of productive capacity).

The principles on which the recoupment period is calculated and the way in which it is used in the calculation of the economic effectiveness of investment provide a good illustration of what is meant by the superiority of a central plan to a market mechanism. They also demonstrate the advantages of employing indirect forms of regulation in the place of direct forms; decisions are taken at a lower level where all the local elements, which it is difficult to take account of centrally, are given their due weight, while all calculations are made with reference to the parameter connecting the micro-economic and macro-economic levels.

The scope and function of the market mechanism are closely connected with the extent to which economic decisions are decentralized. Plainly this means that any attempt to use the market mechanism as an *instrument* of central planning involves the question of the *boundaries of decentralization*. Once again there is no need for a detailed discussion of an issue which has been considered so frequently in Poland; it will suffice to recall the main conclusions.

1. The limits of decentralization are determined by the need to take a group of basic macro-economic decisions, especially those dealing with long-term development, directly at the centre. These questions are chiefly concerned with the division of the national income between accumulation and consumption, the determination of the main areas of investment, the distribution of consumption

income between different groups of the population, etc. From an economic point of view, it is especially important to ensure central control of the basic flow of investment outlays. This is not something which can be settled by some mechanical division of investment into centralized and decentralized (e.g., by fixing the ratio as, say, 70 : 30); the central authorities must be sure of being able decisively to affect the size and structure of the growth of productive capacities. The establishment of definite proportions for the division of investment would need to take into account, as in other analogous problems, among other things, the transmission capacity of the information system, the data-processing capacity of the central authority, the probability of distortions, and the cost of supplying information for differing degrees of centralization.

2. The limits of decentralization are also determined by the centrally determined rules of behaviour for each of the economic units which have been discussed. It is impossible, as we know, to rely on the 'natural' objective functions of enterprises, and it is necessary to lay down objective functions for the sub-systems using criteria drawn from a consideration of the system as a whole. The central authority, at the same time as it lays down the governing rules of behaviour, must also prescribe, at least in outline, the rules determining the connection between the economic results of enterprises (measured according to the rule laid down) and the incomes of its employees. The central authority must be able to ensure that the wage fund is compatible both with market equilibrium and with the social structure of incomes.

3. The limits of decentralization are, finally, determined, by need to ensure control over the economic parameters of the objective function or the outlay function of the economic units at the lower levels of the pyramid. These parameters are constituted by the prices of manufactured goods and services and by the prices of the factors of production, in the broad sense of this term (together with the system of taxation). In order that prices may be a proper guide for the sub-systems, the parametric character of prices ought to be maintained and they ought to express the preferences of society as a whole. It follows that when these conditions cannot be fulfilled it may be necessary to resort to intervention by directives; but, of

course, if the logic of this mechanism for the functioning of the economy is to be maintained, then such action should be exceptional.

These three points add nothing new to the conception of the decentralized model ('the model of a planned economy applying a regulated market mechanism') which I have described elsewhere.[6] In my opinion they show that the assumptions of the decentralized model satisfy the requirement that commodity relations should be subordinated to the essential features and the tendencies of development of a planned socialist economy—in contrast to the tendency towards making commodity relations absolute, discussed in section III above.

## V

In addition to the problem of the limits of decentralization, which is essentially a question concerning economic relations in socialist sectors of the economy, there is also the problem of the scope of commodity relations regarding the spread of total consumption.

The distribution of the basic part of the consumption fund is achieved through the creation of incomes for, and their expenditure by, individual members of the population. Some of the consumption fund, however, is used for social consumption. Without for the moment going into the complicated question of classification (on which there is an increasingly abundant literature, abroad as well as in Poland), it is clear that the role of commodity relations in a socialist system also depends on the way in which consumption is divided between that which is financed by personal incomes and that which is financed out of social funds.

The course of the development of the consumption pattern since the October Revolution is, from this point of view, to some extent analogous to that followed by commodity relations in a socialized economy. Initially (even ignoring the exceptional requirements of the civil war in the USSR), a very large section of consumption was financed from public funds. Later, however, the part played by collective consumption began to diminish and whole areas of consumption were either diverted to private payment (transport and

[6] See *The market in a socialist economy*, London & Boston, 1972.

a number of communal services) or the participation of private payment in the financing of the provision of various goods and services was increased. There has been a particularly striking increase in private payments for accommodation (the development of building co-operatives, an increase in rents) but there have also been other areas in which private payment became increasingly important (e.g., medical care), although less obviously so.

It would be an over-simplification to say that the change in the way in which consumption has been financed has been only in one direction. This would not be true of the last decade, at least in Poland and the USSR, where the proportion of collective consumption in total consumption has not fallen but slightly increased. But this levelling-out, or even increase in the share of collective consumption, has been achieved not so much by an increase in the social financing of particular services, as by the granting of social benefits to groups of the population previously denied them. Hence, among those groups who have always enjoyed some benefits of collective consumption, especially the working class, there has been a feeling that collective consumption has stagnated or even diminished. At all events the policy on collective consumption laid down by the XXII Congress of the Communist Party of the Soviet Union has not been clearly reflected in the development of the socialist countries of Eastern Europe. As far as the Soviet Union itself is concerned, in 1970 the gap between programme and results was very wide.

There is, therefore, in the European socialist countries a large, and, in some sectors, an increasing area in which commodity relations prevail. This can be explained by a number of reasons, some of a temporary nature (for example, difficulty in ensuring market equilibrium as the purchasing power of the population increases). There is no doubt, however, that some of this is due to the argument that there are advantages in developing commodity forms to meet consumer needs (adaptation of the level of demand to the capacity of the economy, increase in freedom of choice in consumption, greater ease with which the real preferences of the population may be ascertained, more effective utilization of capacities as a result of the better use of the services rendered, etc.). The basic argument for transferring several areas from collective consumqtion to consumption from personal incomes is the supposed impetus that this would give to a system of economic incentives (consumption financed out of personal income coupled with a principle of distribution according to labour inputs, as opposed to collective consumption which lacks this tie).

It would be wrong to deny that there is some force in this argument. The establishment of the ratio of collective to individual consumption (and hence how far market forms and non-market forms should be employed in satisfying the needs of the people) is, both as far as the aggregates are concerned and with regard to the particular sectors affected, a very complicated problem to which there is no simple, finite answer. At the same time there is no doubt that the generalization of these arguments and their one-sided employment to support a continual increase in the use of commodity forms for satisfying consumer needs would also be a kind of commodity fetishism.

Non-market forms for satisfying needs are an expression of the *principle of solidarity*, the mutual assistance of members of society in situations where the individual cannot cope with his difficulties on his own. In this sense the highly developed forms of social security are an important element in social integration. If the problem were, however, nothing more than this, then one would expect, with the increase in social affluence and the feeling of security, that the collective consumption fund would shrink to almost nothing. However, the significance of non-market forms in satisfying needs is not confined to a sort of social philanthropy. They have an enormous part to play both as factors of the long-term growth of the economy at a macro-economic level and also as a principle of that collective social life which is part of the political programme of socialism.

Some needs have to be financed from social funds in order to ensure that in areas where investment involves important long-term social benefits but where the outlays are beyond the resources of individual economic units and the rewards lie outside their time preferences, the necessary funds are forthcoming. In some cases the economies of scale and the external economies are so huge that the satisfaction of needs in terms of individual wants is simply not possible (e.g., the counteracting of epidemics, the establishment of the basic elements of the communal infrastructure and the infrastructure of transport). But even in those sectors which can be financed either publicly or privately (general and professional education, medical care, social insurance, etc.) economies of scale, external economies and the dispersion of risk are so important, and the purely consumption side (e.g., education as a good in itself) so closely intertwined with the investment side (education as the increase of productive capacities) that the need to ensure the effective mobilization and exploitation of these long-term factors of economic growth requires that public funds should play the largest part in providing these services.

The social importance of the non-market forms can be divided into two groups of issues. The first is the part to be played by public resources in creating a socially rational structure of consumption. The second is the role of public resources in compensating for the inequalities of income which are bound to arise. Both these sets of problems are closely connected.

The decision to finance from public funds part of the resources available for consumption limits individual households in their choice of consumer goods and services. But it is precisely this limitation (the complete elimination of choice by gratuitous provision or the partial elimination of choice by subsidized prices) which may justify the use of non-market forms of satisfying needs when social and individual preferences diverge to such an extent that to leave the provision of such services to individual choice would endanger the satisfaction of socially important needs. It follows from what has been said above that conflicts of this type are more or less unavoidable and this is also one of the basic factors justifying the use of other than market forms of distribution of consumer goods and services. In a socialist economy the aim is not only to ensure immediate and short-term changes in the composition of consumption but to achieve long-term goals—the development of consumption patterns appropriate to the aspirations of a socialist society—patterns of consumption which it is not easy to foster by the use of the market mechanism.

The redistribution effects of the non-market forms of the satisfaction of needs result from access to benefits independently of income level or, as sometimes happens, from an inverse relationship between access to benefits and income level (goods and services from public resources for low-income groups). In such cases, the corresponding part of the consumption fund is really a factor weakening incentive; but, in compensation, some social groups which would not otherwise do so are able to gain access to certain sectors of consumption. The more egalitarian distribution so achieved is really what might be called a Pigou effect (the utility of a marginal increase in consumption for lower-income groups is greater than the loss for higher-income groups), and there are socio-political advantages as well. The egalitarian provision of collective consumption is exceptionally important in ensuring equality of opportunity in education; it helps to counteract the disadvantages imposed on children by differences between the incomes of their parents.

It is perhaps unnecessary to elaborate on the advantages of this kind of collective consumption. It must be emphasized, however, that the egalitarian effect of collective consumption is due not so much to the fact of its existence, but arises from the way in which services are financed and the way in which benefits are distributed. Indeed, situations may arise in which, accidentally or otherwise, the collective provision of goods and services results in an increase of income differentiation—a relatively high personal income may also coincide with a relatively high participation in social benefits. I am not referring to the open, though difficult to quantify, privileges linked with the occupation of an important position in the socio-political hierarchy, but to the easier access to certain kinds of social benefit which results from advantages conferred in the past. This phenomenon is particularly striking with regard to the availability of higher education. Children brought up in better material circumstances than others have a better chance of reaching a better than average level of education, which is to say that they receive a disproportionate and, in some cases, extremely disproportionate share, of the public funds devoted to education. As far as the educational system is concerned this is a matter of particular importance. What we have here may become the inheritance of specific capital— educational capital—and this may lead to the petrification of particular social strata and to the loss of talent through neglect. This is why it is important to have a conscious policy not only for the division

63

of consumption between the individual and the collective, but also for deciding the apportionment of payments and the distribution of benefits. Neither aspect of the problem can be resolved by relying on the market.

This article is not concerned with the problem of private enterprise in socialist countries but in passing it is worth noting that a more pronounced and more effective policy of income distribution would have an effect on private enterprise far greater than that of its immediate economic consequences. Excessively high incomes in the least controlled area of commodity relations have a psychological effect; this may be a not unimportant source of ideology related to commodity fetishism.

This apart, what I have been trying to say is that one of the most important things to remember when employing the market mechanism in a planned socialist economy is that the *commercial provision of consumer goods and services must be limited*. A failure to do so would be to fall victim to commodity fetishism.


## VI

It follows from our sketch of the nature and scope of commodity relations in socialism that a socialist society—being a modern society—must make centrally a number of basic macro-economic choices. Apart from taking some direct substantive decisions the central authority must also lay down the powers of the subordinate organizations and be able to define *the limits of decentralization*, the 'rules of the game' for the autonomous units of the lower levels of the pyramid (sub-systems), and the boundaries within which the *commercial provision of consumer goods and services* must be confined.

The exercise of choice for these purposes is, in the nature of things, a political act—both the substance of the decisions and the criteria employed are political. The substance of the decisions is political because the fundamental macro-economic choices depend on some kind of compromise between various conflicting social interests and between the conflicting interests of different social groups. In general, there is no way of resolving these conflicts so that all interests will be equally satisfied. Macro-economic decisions are political in nature because the criteria are not given externally but are derived from the system itself and are based on some set of values; optimization in terms of the national economy as a whole is only a solution to a particular goal or set of goals and must, therefore, depend on internally derived criteria of value.

The description of macro-economic decisions as 'political' is sometimes regarded with suspicion by those who fear that the effect of the adjective is to reduce the importance of choices made by the central authorities by substituting for them decisions made with reference to 'objective' market criteria. It is quite clear that the term 'political' has here no pejorative implication, but simply reflects the fact that macro-economic choices—precisely because of the scale of their implications and their independence of current market indices—must be arrived at in a different way from the decisions made by individual economic units. It is, in any case, easy to understand why some autocrats have so fiercely denied that the decisions they take are political; it is simply much more convenient to introduce them as the direct result of objective necessity and hence as decisions which are *a priori* the best and indeed the only ones possible.

It follows from the assertion that the basic macro-economic decisions are political that the cardinal problem in creating and developing socialist relations of production, the construction of 'a society of free associations of producers', is how to ensure real social participation in, and control of, these decisions. In our present situation, this is a problem of state, of *the system for the exercise of political power.*

I do not consider that this invalidates the proposition that the ownership of the means of production determines the type of economic relations in an economy. Political power and the control of the means of production are inseparable in a socialist system, they cannot be considered in isolation from each other. This is of basic importance for the proper understanding of the *process* of the socialization of the means of production—a process which lies at the heart of the development of a socialist society.

In the Polish literature the idea that socialization is a process was forcefully expounded by Edward Lipiński: 'The socialization of the means of production is a process, not a fact. This process is complete when the working man ceases to treat his production task as a private affair. Only when there is a genuine co-management of the means of production which he exploits is there a genuine ˎsocialization of the means of production.'[7] The connection between this idea, the theory of commodity fetishism and the overcoming of alienation is clear.

Lipiński attaches great importance to the decentralization of decisions as an effective way 'of overcoming the contradictions between the individual and the social tasks of production'. 'It is possible', he writes, 'that the decentralization of management, the transfer even to the smallest groups of the task of taking decisions about the broadest technical and human problems involved in the groups' activities would provide a new and realistic road to the conquest of alienation.'[8]

It is difficult to deny that the decentralization of decisions, justified in terms of the greater efficiency and lower cost of information flows, is of fundamental significance in the creation of a feeling of genuine co-management of the means of production, especially if it is accompanied by the development of workers' self-government. Hence the hopes focused on economic reforms in Eastern European countries— hopes for not purely economic but also for socio-political effects for transformations of the model. But these changes cannot of themselves provide an answer unless one is prepared to treat the socialist economy as a collective commodity economy in which, in the last instance, the macro-economic decisions are the resultant of autonomous individual decisions. If, however, the results of our analysis are accepted, and the *limits* of decentralization as well as the functions of the market mechanism are clearly defined, while it is plainly understood that certain macro-economic decisions must be taken autonomously by the central authorities, then the solution of the problem will not be sought in decentralization alone. The solution must be sought, first of all, by ensuring the real participation of society in *the taking of decisions at the centre*, that is, by a genuine democratization of the system for the exercise of state power. The *process* of the socialization of the means of production must be at the same time

[7] Edward Lipiński, op. cit., p. 190.
[8] Ibid., p. 205.

the withering-away of the state, in the sense intended by Lenin: 'The more democratic the "State", which consists of armed workers, and which is "no longer a state in the proper sense of the word", the more rapidly *every form* of state begins to wither away.'[9]

Unless the process of socialization makes progress the *socialist* factor in integration, the feeling that there is co-management of the means of production, will weaken. There may also be attempts to replace the socialist integrating elements by others, like nationalism or even racism, the results of which, especially in the long term, are disastrous. The 'socialism of idiots' as August Bebel once described anti-semitism, always leads to the development of an apparatus of coercion and the suppression of free speech, setting up 'feedbacks' which, with the passage of time, may be very difficult to correct without considerable social damage.

The criteria described in this essay are not, and cannot be, used in an assessment of the way in which the political institutions of contemporary socialist countries operate, although as the socialist societies of today attain a higher material and intellectual level these criteria will assume increasing importance. However, if one accepts this theory of commodity fetishism as a general theory of the fetishism of all forms of social relations, then it is clear that the primary task of the social sciences in a socialist system is to make a careful and thorough *analysis of the present political institutions comparing their form with their real content.* Marxism has never contented itself with the superficial description of social phenomena—it has always sought out the intrinsic relationships concealed under their external forms. There is no substantive reason why such an approach should not be adopted towards the dialectic of form and content in a system of socialist relations of production and towards one of the most important elements in socialist production relations, the political system.

'It may well be thought', writes Edward Lipiński, 'that mystification is a recurrent phenomenon in history and that it makes its appearance wherever the defence of an entrenched position requires the mystification of reality.'[10] Socialism cannot claim exemption

[9] V. I. Lenin, *Selected works*, London, 1969, p. 337.
[10] Op. cit., p. 235.

from this rule and the Marxist theory of commodity fetishism has still an important and stimulating role to play. This is especially true of its significance as a critique of the fetishism of forms—in this case, the fetishism of the institutions of a political system.

[First published in *Politique d'aujourd'hui*, nos 11 and 12, 1969.]

# 5 | Economic calculus and political decisions

## I

The importance of political decisions for economic developments increases with the growth in the part played in the economy by the state. An increase in the role of the state means that instead of macro-economic processes being the result of micro-economic activity, general considerations play a more and more important part in economic decisions. For obvious reasons the significance of these factors is particularly great in a socialist economy and this is what gives the examination of the interrelationship between economy and politics its special importance.

In the period of socialist history which runs from 1929 to 1956, a period which has still to be fully assessed, economic developments were under immense pressure from political decisions, although throughout the period it was always maintained that policy was determined not by political but by economic regularities. The choice of one economic policy rather than another was supposed to be determined always and uniquely by economic laws. The role of political economy—as some of us know from our own experience—consisted in the exposition of these laws so as to provide a pseudo-scientific explanation of actual economic practice.

The current tendency to exclude anything political from economics is a reaction against that state of affairs. The search for optimal solutions is supposed to be based exclusively on economic calculus and to consist in the absolutely objective analysis of the relationships between economic aggregates presented in an increasingly complex mathematical form. It is difficult to deny that the emphasis placed on economic calculus is one of the more important signs of the tendency to rationality in economics or that improved methods of this calculus should play an important part in solving both the short- and long-term problems of our economy. But while recognizing the importance of all this it should also be remembered:

... what it is that we may really expect from economic calculus in its strict sense;

... the limits within which decisions may be made solely on the basis of economic calculus;

... the nature of the part played by political factors in economic calculus and what sort of mechanism is needed to ensure the sychronization of all these elements in the decision-taking process.

It is these problems with which this chapter is concerned, although it must be emphasized that it is nothing more than an extremely simplified outline sketch; much less than is needed for a comprehensive analysis. I shall make use of examples of alternatives of choice of the kind discussed in the Polish literature dealing with the theory of growth and especially in the work of Kalecki.[1] I want to stress that I am using them as simplified illustrations and not as theoretical proofs. More important, the example chosen is not offered as the only strategy for accelerating the rate of growth but is simply one of a number of possibilities which provide an especially clear demonstration of the relationship between economic calculus and political decision.

## II

One of the requirements before any economic calculus can be made is the definition of the objective function, i.e., the definition and quantification of the effect for which an optimal solution is sought. Let us suppose that we are trying to maximize consumption.

This aim already has a political content. It is true that the maximization of consumption might well be considered as a natural aim for economic activity in a socialist system but:

1. at some periods this aim may stand lower in the scale of priorities than other goals (e.g., social reconstruction, the maximization of armament production, etc.);

2. the maximization of consumption can be interpreted in different ways:

... as the maximization of consumption per head of the population,

[1] Michał Kalecki, *Introduction to the theory of growth in a socialist economy*, Oxford, 1969. See also Kazimierz Łaski, *Zarys teorii reprodukcji socjalistycznej (An outline of the theory of socialist reproduction)*, Warsaw, 1965.

... as the maximization of a real wage, i.e., the maximization of individual consumption per person employed,

... as the maximization of either of these two indices subject or not to certain constraints (e.g., for given changes in income differentials, a given ratio between individual and collective consumption), etc.

At the outset then we are faced with a political decision—the definition of the objective function and the choice of the indices in terms of which it shall be measured. Until we have made such a decision we cannot decide what is the optimal allocation of resources.

Let us suppose that we have taken our initial political decision and we have decided that the long-term aim of the plan is the maximization of total consumption, which means, supposing that the growth of population is independent of this decision, the maximization of consumption per head of the population. What is now the basis of our economic calculus and what part is played in it by political factors? In answering this problem we shall make use of the schematic example to which we referred above.

Let us suppose, that in the period preceding the point at which we must choose between compatible variants of the plan, the national income is increasing at a rate of 10 per cent per unit of time, that the rate of investment is 20 per cent and that the capital-output ratio is constant and equals 2.[2] This rate of investment secures a 5 per cent rate of growth in employment (it is assumed that this equals the growth of the working population), and technical progress gives a rate of increase of labour productivity of 5 per cent. Obviously, on our assumptions, consumption (which here, in another simplification, equals national income minus investment) also increases steadily at 10 per cent per unit of time, since the share of consumption in the national income remains unchanged; when 20 per cent of the national

---

[2] For the sake of simplicity we exclude non-investment factors and employ the simplified formula

$$r = i \cdot \frac{1}{m}$$

where $r$ = the rate of growth of the national income, $i$ = the rate of investment (the share of investment in the national income), $m$ = the capital-output ratio (the amount of investment outlay required for a unit of increment in the national income).

income is devoted to investment, 80 per cent will be given over to consumption.

Let us now suppose that the planning authorities are considering whether the rate of growth can be increased in order to increase consumption both aggregate and per head of the population. It is not possible to accelerate growth by increasing the rate of growth of employment because the increase in the working population is given. It is possible, however, to increase the rate of growth of labour productivity by a higher degree of mechanization in newly installed (or modernized) projects, i.e., by using more capital-intensive techniques of production. In the period of transition to a higher capital-output ratio, the rate of growth of labour productivity will be higher than the previous rate of 5 per cent and consequently the rate of growth of national income will be increased. Once a higher capital-output ratio and labour productivity have been reached, a new level of mechanization will be established and we shall return to the old 'natural' growth rate of labour productivity and the national income. But we shall have gained a permanent advantage in terms of national income and the level of labour productivity, since the growth rate, although the same as that with which we started, is now a percentage of a larger absolute amount.

Let, for example, labour productivity at a particular moment equal 10 units of the national income (reckoned always in constant prices) per worker. Then, at a constant capital-output ratio, in the second period labour productivity will increase by 5 per cent as a result of technical progress, and will equal 10·5 units. If, however, the capital-output ratio is raised, labour productivity will increase in the second period to, say, 11 units of national income per employee, i.e., the rate of growth of labour productivity in the second period will equal 10 per cent (5 per cent due to technical progress and an extra 5 per cent due to replacing less by more capital-intensive techniques). If the level of the capital-output ratio is not raised any further, labour productivity will increase in successive periods only as a result of technical progress, i.e., by 5 per cent. None the less, 5 per cent of 11 is more than 5 per cent of 10·5, and so on. Thus, the *level* of labour productivity, and consequently the *level* of the national income will be higher in a more capital-intensive variant than in a less capital-intensive variant, although the *rate* of growth will be higher only in the transitional period while the more capital-intensive method is being introduced, and will then return to its original level.

In the interests of strict accuracy it should be noted that the example given assumes *neutral technical progress* (as defined in chapter 7 of Kalecki's book). I have also given a very simplified account of the transitional period. It is assumed, for instance, that the entire national income is produced in new plants resulting from putting into operation successive investment projects. In reality, the productive apparatus consists of a number of 'vintages', which implies that the transition to a higher level of capital intensity cannot take place at once but develops gradually as old equipment is replaced by new. In growth theory (see chapters 7 and 8 in Kalecki's book), this is described as the 'recasting' of the productive apparatus from one capital intensity ratio into another. The rate of 'recasting' is crucial to the rate of growth in the 'transitional period'; but I shall not go into this here because it does not affect our conclusions.

A change from a lower to a higher level of capital-output ratio must therefore always be favourable in terms of growth of the national income (assuming, obviously, rational behaviour; i.e., it is excluded as absurd that an increase in capital-output ratio will have no positive effect on labour productivity). But is it so obvious that it will be equally favourable in terms of growth of consumption?

Let us begin at the end. So far, from what we have said, it follows that, having completed this transition, the higher the level of capital-output ratio at which we arrive, the higher the level of the national income achieved; thereafter, whatever the value of the capital-output ratio, there will be the same ('natural') rate of growth of the national income. But it follows from the relationship between the rate of growth, the rate of investment and the capital-output ratio that the same rate of growth coupled with a higher capital-output ratio requires a higher share of investment in the national income. Obviously, a higher rate of investment, *ceteris paribus*, entails a lower rate of consumption. At the end of the transitional period, therefore, the rate of consumption is equivocal: the higher the capital-output ratio, the higher the national income, but the lower the share of it devoted to consumption. Everything depends on which of the two factors is dominant.

Returning to our numerical illustration, let us assume that, at a capital-output ratio of 2 and at a rate of investment of 20 per cent, the initial level of the national income equals 1,000, i.e., consumption is 800. If development proceeds at this capital coefficient, then, after a certain time (corresponding to the time required for a possible 'recasting'), the national income will reach, say, 1,200 and consumption 960 units (variant A). The planning authorities might, however, adopt other variants of development. Let us assume the following characteristic of variant B: capital coefficient of 2·3; level of national income after completion of the acceleration manoeuvre, 1,300; rate of investment necessary to maintain a 10 per cent rate of growth, 23 per cent rate of consumption, 77 per cent; hence, the level of consumption at the end of the transition process, 1,000 units approximately. Let us consider three other variants (C, D, E), each with a higher capital-output ratio. These variants are set out in the following table.

Table of national income, capital investment and consumption rates

|  | A | B | C | D | E |
|---|---|---|---|---|---|
| National income after completion of the manœuvre | 1,200 | 1,300 | 1,380 | 1,430 | 1,460 |
| Capital-output ratio | 2·0 | 2·3 | 2·6 | 3·0 | 3·5 |
| Investment rate (%) needed to maintain a 10% growth rate | 20 | 23 | 26 | 30 | 35 |
| Rate of consumption (%) | 80 | 77 | 74 | 70 | 65 |
| Total consumption (approximate figures) after completion of the manœuvre | 960 | 1,000 | 1,020 | 1,000 | 950 |

Each successive variant gives a higher level of national income for a higher level of the capital-output ratio, but not every variant gives a higher level of consumption. Maximum consumption is given by variant C. Variant D gives a higher level of consumption than the original variant A, but lower than C, in spite of the higher capital-output ratio. Variant E, which gives the highest level of national income, gives a lower level of consumption than all the other variants, including the initial variant A. It is important to remember that unless there is some change in development strategy *the characteristics of the individual variant remain unchanged*: ever since completion of the manœuvre, variant E will always give the highest level of national income and the lowest level of consumption, variant C will always give the highest level of consumption, etc., since for every level of national income, investment and consumption will rise, period on period, at *a rate of 10 per cent*.

### III

What conclusions are to be drawn from this analysis?

First, not every increase in the growth rate will, in the long run, increase consumption. This is a very important result because it is often supposed that while an increase in the rate of growth may have an adverse effect on consumption in the short term, in the long run consumption always gains. Variant E shows, however, a case where the loss in terms of current consumption is not compensated by a subsequent increase in consumption in the long run because the capital-output ratio of the methods chosen is too high.

Second, if one variant for accelerating growth increases consumption in the long run, this does not absolve the planner from comparing it with other variants. For example, variant D gives a better consumption effect than variant A, but is less effective than variant C, although D is more expensive than C (in terms of the higher capital-output ratio). The consumption effects of B and D are identical but the rate of investment needed for D is higher. It follows that D should be rejected. If, as a result of past erroneous calculations, the capital-output ratio had been increased too much and we found ourselves in situation D (or, even worse, E), then the maximization of consumption would require a retreat, i.e., not an acceleration, but a deceleration of growth, by 'recasting' towards a lower capital-output ratio.

Both these results are based on purely economic calculations (but calculations made for a given objective function—maximization of consumption). If the aim is different (e.g., the maximization of production over a long period) the conclusions will be different: for this purpose variant E is better than variant C.

None the less, assuming that our aim is the maximization of consumption, is it the case that C may be adopted as the optimum solution? Not at all. One must also take into account what happens in the period of transition from one capital-output ratio to another. Compared with A and B, variant C gives a higher level of consumption in the long run, but requires a higher rate of investment during the transitional period and hence greater sacrifices in present consumption. This does not, of course, necessarily mean an absolute fall in the level of consumption, but, absolute or relative, the fall is greater than in the case of A or B. This is the classic contradiction between short-term and long-term advantage. The planner cannot resolve this contradiction by the use of strictly economic calculus. Economic calculus makes it possible to reject those variants which fail to maximize the objective function (here, variants D and E) and indicates the range of possible solutions (in our case, variants C, B, and A, which satisfy the condition that a current sacrifice in consumption is more than compensated by the long-term effect on consumption). The choice between C, B, and A requires the use of non-economic criteria—the assessment of how far present advantages should be sacrificed to future advantages. This is, of course, a political decision. A choice must be made between variant C which gives the best long-term result (corresponding to the 'golden rule of accumulation'), variant B with its less ambitious programme for growth, and A, which does not entail an increase in the growth rate at all but entails no reduction in current consumption.

In making a political assessment between the relative 'value' of present and future advantages a vital consideration would be one's judgment of the effect of a particular economic strategy on the attitude of those engaged in economic activity, i.e., on the productivity of labour and the general efficiency of the system. We shall not discuss this problem here but its importance is obvious.

Let us now attempt to sum up. Some of the elements in what I have been saying have, for the purposes of illustration, been presented in a very simplified form. But the general conclusions are clear.

On the one hand, there is no doubt about the importance of economic calculus in eliminating ineffective solutions and demarcating the area within which acceptable solutions are to be found. To ignore economic calculus and the theories on which it is based, and to replace them by rigid *a priori* dogma or intuition, can only cause losses—the larger the scale of the decisions, the greater the extent of the losses. Methods of economic calculus need, therefore, continual improvement both in their theoretical basis and in the techniques for their application. At the same time—and we shall not discuss this here—the socio-economic preconditions for their application also need to be improved—e.g., by developing an economic system which provides incentives for the application of economic calculus.

Not even this can create ideal conditions, but it will provide increasing precision in the formulation of alternative choices. However, even the greatest precision in the economic calculus will never eliminate (and this is the other aspect of our conclusions) the necessity for making political decisions in drawing up plans of development, because:

1. the initial point of reference (the objective function) is the result of a political decision;

2. the selection of the optimal variant from among a number of possible alternatives arrived at by economic calculation is a political decision;

3. they are political decisions which, in determining the size and composition of the funds available for consumption, indirectly determine the parameters entering economic calculus by their effect on the behaviour of those engaged in economic activity.

It follows that the optimization of economic decisions, in the broad sense of this term, embodies not only the system and techniques of economic calculus but also a corresponding political mechanism within which conflicting interests can be clarified and compromises reached, so that the decisions taken in the name of society are as close as possible to real social preferences. It is very important that the alternatives for development strategy should be presented clearly and openly so that they may be publicly discussed. This requires that there needs to be some sort of 'feedback' between those responsible for taking the decisions and public opinion. This would have two advantages:

. . . on the one hand it would teach society better to identify its long- and short-term interests (provided, of course, that it can be shown that any of the proposed decisions are in their interest);

. . . on the other hand the expression of public opinion with regard to the various alternatives would teach those responsible for political decisions better to identify the exact extent to which society is prepared to sacrifice present for future advantage, a vital factor in deciding on the optimal solution.

A political mechanism of this kind is the necessary precondition for the development of the feeling that the nationalized means of production are being jointly managed, and without this no permanent progress can be expected in a socialist economy.

For economics, all this demonstrates the necessity of a genuine and not merely formal recognition of the interdependence of economic and political decisions. The tendency, at various times and for various reasons to eliminate one of the terms from political economy must be resisted—both elements are equally important, not only because such is the tradition of progressive, and especially Marxist, political economies but, above all, because this is what life demands.

[First published in *Zycie Gospodarcze* (*The Economic Life*, no. 42, Warsaw, 1967.]

# 6 | Political economy and the relationship between economy and politics under socialism

The key element in the Marxist attitude in the social sciences is the emphasis placed on the *active* role assigned to science as the instrument of the progressive transformation of the real world. The active role of science requires that it shall critically analyse the real world, laying bare the contradictions inherent in it and showing how they can be overcome.

It was precisely this attitude which was exemplified in the Marxist political economy of capitalism. The question we are going to consider is this: whether and in what sense the maintenance of this Marxist tradition in the political economy of socialism is a necessary condition for the fulfilment of its active role in the development of socialist society.

## Why the socialist revolution does not mean the end of political economy as a science

Let us begin by recalling that in the course of the development of Marxist economics it was sometimes reckoned that political economy would come to an end at the same time as the capitalist system. Among those holding such views were those whose names are an integral part of the history of Marxism—Hilferding, Bukharin, Rosa Luxemburg.

It would be a naïve over-simplification to object that these great Marxists, in denying the need for a political economy of socialism, were disputing the existence of any kind of objective regularities in the economic process of a socialist system. Nevertheless it seems that they thought the only problems in socialism would be those arising in connection with the development of the productive forces, i.e., technical problems; hence, the only problem facing science would be that of discovering what today, to use Oskar Lange's terminology, we would call the technical-balance laws of production. Some theory would be indispensable, but it would not be political economy which is a theory of *social* laws of production; in socialism, the place of political economy would be taken by a science described by some of the writers mentioned as the theory of the rational organization of productive forces.

Is there nothing of value in such a view? It contains, of course, a number of important elements. Every firm must try as best it can to solve the problems with which it is faced—how to obtain the maximum effect from a given outlay, or how to obtain a given effect from a minimum outlay (the maximization of the objective function or the minimization of the function of the means). A planned economy, based on the nationalization of the means of production, means, in a sense, that these problems have been shifted to the national level. But the Marxian economy of capitalism was not concerned with these problems—it was not a science of rational economic operation under capitalism. Under socialism, however, economics must deal with these problems; it must examine and apply the best possible programming techniques both in calculations dealing with co-ordination and, especially, in the calculation of optimization, i.e., in the selection of the most effective solutions. This opens a wide area for the economic applications of mathematics, cybernetics and other fields of knowledge which enrich the methods of programming and in so doing supply the instruments indispensable for assessing the rationality of economic activity.

It is, however, clear, that *in as far as* the economist concerns himself (and he must so concern himself) with the theory and technique of programming, he is not directly concerned with social problems. The theory and technique of programming is socially neutral; it is concerned with the relationships between means and targets from the two most general points of view: establishing whether a given target is attainable and establishing the conditions for the achievement of a particular target for the smallest possible outlay. These are problems which arise in every sphere of human activity and thus constitute, in their general form, the subject of praxiology—the science of rational activity—i.e., the study of the general rational activity factors and conditions of effective operation.

Social problems arise only when we pass from general considerations concerning targets and means to the concrete definition of the target and the means in the context of some specific economic activity. We are then dealing with something which the theory of programming treats as given.

In order properly to define the means and targets of economic activity, taking full account of objective circumstances and developmental requirements, is there a need, in socialism, for a separate branch of science dealing with the socio-economic, and not just the technical, aspects of the economy? The negative answer to this question stemmed from the conviction that the overthrow of capitalism would mean the removal of all *socio-economic* obstacles to and of all contradictions in the development of the productive forces; the socio-economic problems of socialism would be, as it were, transparent, so that the need for a science concerned to lay bare the reality of things behind the veil of fetishized forms would disappear. In particular, it was considered that socialism, in overcoming the spontaneity of economic development, in reuniting the producers with the means of production and in effecting a direct connection between the interests of the individual and the needs of society, would, at a stroke, create the necessary preconditions for overcoming alienation, the estrangement of man-the-producer from the instruments and products of his own labour.

Again, in this idea, there is a considerable degree of truth. Socialism—especially in its developed form—does indeed overcome the contradictions of capitalism and creates a progressive socio-economic basis for economic development. The nationalization of the basic means of production means that the commercial criteria of rationality in a private economy are replaced by socio-economic criteria which, at the same time, bring about a fundamental change in the position of man in the economic process.

The inexactness, incompleteness, and the inaccuracy of this idea results, in the last analysis, from the fact that it identifies the suppression of the socio-economic contradictions of capitalism with the suppression of contradictions in general. This leads to the assertion that relationships between the means of production and the productive forces in socialism are free from contradictions and fully harmonious. This is, of course, not true. Socialism creates the *preconditions* for overcoming alienation, but these preconditions are nothing more than that; a long road separates the nationalization of the means of production from their complete socialization, the creation of what we often call a socialist attitude to work and social ownership.

And if this is the case, then socialism needs not only a technical theory of economic operation, 'a science of the rational organization of productive forces', but also a political economy in its strict sense, the adjective *political* being given its full force. What is needed is not a theory of economic operation in general, but a social theory of economic activity providing a penetrating analysis of the contradictions in the socialist mode of production and offering a critical account of the ways in which they may be overcome.

## Socialism does not put an end to socio-economic contradictions

The comprehensive characteristic of economic contradictions in socialism is not a simple matter. I have dealt with some aspects of it elsewhere.[1] Here I shall confine myself to the consideration of one problem for the sake of example.

It is said that socialism resolves the contradiction, peculiar to capitalism, between production and consumption. This is true in the sense that the capitalist owner of the means of production is governed by the need to maximize profits while in socialism the purpose of production is the maximization of consumption in society as a whole, a purpose dictated by the social ownership of the means of production. This does not mean, however, that the relationship between production and consumption in socialism is free from contradictions.

First, there is the problem described in economics as that of the 'time horizon'. The growth of consumption over a long period depends critically on the growth of production. The growth of production is connected in turn with the creation of the appropriate productive apparatus and this demands the undertaking of investment. In certain circumstances this leads to a situation in which the drive to increase consumption in the long term limits the growth of consumption in the short term. This has socio-political results, which

[1] *The market in a socialist economy*, London & Boston, 1972.

may in turn have very concrete economic effects. The excessive limitation of current consumption may adversely affect labour productivity and jeopardize the planned increment of production.

Second, the growth of consumption may be achieved in various ways with correspondingly varied social consequences. For example, the growth of consumption achieved principally by an increase in employment is not the same as a growth in consumption achieved principally as a result of an increase in productivity. The same increase in the goods available for consumption is much more weakly reflected in the growth of real wages (per man employed) in the former case than in the latter.

Third, the growth of consumption may take the form of an increase in individual or in social consumption.[2]

Fourth, the increase in consumption may be variously distributed between different social classes and strata and the way in which the growth of consumption is distributed may itself affect the size of the consumption fund. This problem is closely connected with the problem of income differentiation and hence with a series of complicated socio-economic problems usually described as the problem of 'egalitarianism *versus* the differentiation of incomes' in socialism.

## The need for a mechanism of choice between socio-economic alternatives

This handful of problems drawn from only one area is enough to enable one to realize what a vast variety of possibilities are concealed behind the apparently simple and uniformly conceived purpose of production in socialism. It is at the same time quite clear that these different possibilities are not technical, but socio-economic, alternatives and hence that the choice of solution must be calculated with reference to various current and long-term interests and factors. Political economy can play its indispensable—active—role in determining the development of a socialist society only if it can show up the socio-economic contradictions which actually appear in the

[2] By 'social consumption' is meant the consumption of goods and services provided by the state for the population as a whole in the form of education, social services, pensions, etc.

economic process and therefore demonstrate the directions to be taken and the mechanism to be employed in resolving them.

Both these questions—that of the directions to be taken and of the mechanism to be adopted—are of fundamental significance. The process of overcoming alienation consists in a growing identification of personal interests with the interests of society. This means, among other things, that politico-economic forms must be created which will assist in laying bare and resolving the dialectical contradictions in a socialist economy. This is connected with the problem of the relationship between the economy and politics in socialism which will be discussed below. However, even now it is possible to state with absolute certainty that, for example, a concrete economic plan consisting of an ordered set of decisions dealing with the basic economic problems in a given period ought never to be considered as the absolute solution from every point of view (which is in general impossible) but as one out of a number of possible choices. And if this is so, then, in order to ensure real social participation in the discussions of the plan, it is necessary to set out the alternatives plainly and clearly, showing the advantages and disadvantages of each, so making it possible for the various views to be clarified and subjected to a full analysis. This is one of the sources of the demand that the long-term plan should be prepared and discussed not, as hitherto, in one, but in several versions.

Analogous problems arise in connection with the rules of the operation of a socialist economy. The organizational rules of a planned economy—the scope of centralization and decentralization and of direct administrative and market instruments, the role of economic incentives—ought to be regarded as a particular development in the socialist mode of production. Happily, the view that there is one, and only one, form of economic mechanism appropriate to a socialist economy is now a thing of the past. This is the root of the basic economic task—the choice of forms corresponding to the conditions of a given period of development. This task is all the more momentous now that the European socialist countries are entering a stage in which factors of intensive growth are predominant. The exploitation of these factors demands a much greater subtlety and precision in the directing of the economy and increasing participation by the masses in management, the full exploitation of the potential possibilities of which are inherent in the still imperfect organs of workers' self-government.

## The political preconditions for the development of political economy under socialism

Under socialism, therefore, *political* economy is indispensable—a full-blooded social science continuing the true Marxian traditions. This does not weaken the significance of the development of economic programming: the search for, and perfection of, methods which allow a better understanding and development of the technical production side of rational economic operation.

The creation of a social theory of economic operation, however, demands more than the formal recognition of the need for political economy as such. The views which we mentioned at the outset of this article have long belonged to the past. Nevertheless, although the political economy of socialism has for several decades occupied an honourable position among Marxist social disciplines, it is still difficult to enthuse about its present role in the development of a socialist society. This is perhaps due to the fact that in the course of a relatively long period of time the formal recognition of its function was accompanied by circumstances in which one of the most fundamental aspects of the Marxian tradition was frustrated: a critical approach to politico-economic phenomena was impossible. A discipline which, instead of laying bare the real contradictions in the developmental process, conceals them in the name of universal harmony, loses all hope of affecting the real world and transforms itself from science into apologetics. In the past, unfortunately, the political economy of socialism has not escaped this fate. The disastrous consequences of this can be found, for example, in the conviction of some economists that the only field for positive action is to be found in the formal theory of programming, organization, and so on. Consequently, the term 'social theory of economic operation' still represents a proposition rather than a reality. It is not difficult to imagine the negative results of this state of affairs on the understanding of the processes of economic development under socialism and hence on the policies adopted.

A change in this situation depends on many factors—also on the attitudes of the social *engagement* of, and the intellectual freedom afforded to, economists themselves. There is no doubt, however, that the initial condition for the development of the political economy of socialism as a social theory of economic operation is the creation of a political climate in which the critical analysis of the real world and the independent search for solutions is treated as meritorious activity, and not as an infraction of the general line. Certain political preconditions are indispensable for the development of political economy.

## The modification of the relationship between economy and politics under socialism

In our discussion we have so far glanced at the problems of the relationship between economy and politics under socialism from various angles. In this there is, of course, nothing remarkable, since the correct definition of this relationship is one of the fundamental premisses of *political* economy *sensu stricto*.

We can formulate the problem as follows: is it correct to suppose—as is the general practice either explicitly or implicitly in Marxist literature—that the relationship between the economic base and the political superstructure under socialism is analogous, at least as far as its general properties are concerned, with that found in other socio-economic forms?

In the work of Polish sociologists and economists dealing with the general principles of historical development the ownership of the means of production is recognized, without reservation, as the basic element in the relations of production. Oskar Lange's formulation is typical: 'The ownership of the means of production is, so to speak, the organizing principle which determines the relations of productions in their entirety.'[3] At the same time the state—according to

[3] Oskar Lange, *Political economy*, Oxford, 1963, vol. 1, p. 72. In passing it should be noted that the idea of ownership as the fundamental category which determines all other aspects of production relations is sometimes criticized by those who advocate what may be called a functional concept of ownership. According to this view, ownership is not a separate and fundamental category but is the expression of the whole configuration of the relations of distribution, co-operation, the relative positions of individual

Marx's famous formulation in his Preface to *A Contribution to the Critique of Political Economy*—is considered a part of the super-structure, which rises above the 'foundations of economic life',[4] and adapts itself to the economic base according to 'the law of the necessary agreement between the superstructure and the economic base' (i.e. the so-called second fundamental sociological law[5]). Each of these two elements, the ownership of the means of production and the state (political power), is the object of thorough separate analysis and its significance under socialism carefully considered. However, the nature of their mutual relationship—on the one hand as 'base' and hence the determining factor, and on the other hand as 'superstructure' and hence as the determined factor—is generally accepted and regarded as holding good also under socialism. It seems to me that this conviction, if I understand it correctly, is ill founded. In my opinion, the traditionally accepted relationship between economy and policy as 'base' on the one hand, and 'superstructure' on the other and hence as, 'in the last resort', the determining factor and the determined factor, needs, with respect to socialism, fundamental modification. Economy and politics are so intimately intertwined, especially when considered dynamically, that the continued use of the old conceptual apparatus of 'base' and 'superstructure' becomes more and more inadequate. The dependence of the further development of socialist relations of production, and hence of the evolution of the 'economic base', on a corresponding development in political relationships—on changes in the political power system—makes itself especially felt in periods of crisis.

This alteration in the relationship between economy and politics is evident in the very definition of a socialist economic system. The basic characteristic of such a system is generally reckoned to be the predominance of the social ownership of the means of production. (We shall not deal here with the difference between state and

---

social classes and groups, etc. See *Ekonomika, zajmy, politika* (*Economics, interests, politics*) by the Czech economist Ota Šik, Prague, 1962.

[4] See Zygmunt Bauman, *Zarys socjologii* (*An outline of sociology*), Warsaw, 1962, p. 184, and Maria Hirszowicz, *Konfrontacje socjologiczne* (*Sociological confrontations*), Warsaw, 1964, chapter IV.

[5] Oskar Lange, op. cit., vol. I, p. 30.

co-operative ownership but assume that we are concerned with social ownership appearing nowadays in the form of state ownership.)

What, however, is social ownership? It is surprisingly difficult to find a full and precise definition of this term in the handbooks of historical materialism and the political economy of socialism.

Joseph Schumpeter[6] along with many other non-Marxist authors uses the term *public ownership*, a concept at least partly derived from the formal and legal difference between the property of public bodies (the state, local government, etc.) and the property of private individuals or private organizations. It should be noted that even when so defined, in a socio-economic system where public ownership dominates, the relationship between politics and the economy is already quite different from that which obtains in classical capitalism, since now the political factor directly influences economic decisions about the growth and distribution of the national income.

Marxist literature, however, has never been satisfied with the definition of social ownership as public ownership. Public ownership (especially state ownership) is not considered to be social ownership if it occurs in a capitalist state. The socialist character of the state is a necessary condition for the recognition of public ownership as social ownership. Hence, in this case, the *character* of the state—a political institution, an element in the superstructure—is considered to be a factor determining a basic relation of production—the nature of the ownership of the means of production.[7]

Of course it is easy to show that the rise of the socialist state (and hence the socialist political revolution) is, in the last analysis, determined by the development of economic relations within the capitalist

[6] *Capitalism, Socialism and Democracy*, 7th ed., London, 1957. There is not room here for a full analysis of his views. But Schumpeter, one of the few theoreticians of socio-economic development in its broadest sense, holds that the transition to socialist economy is a regular feature of the development of society. His concept, even though it deviates from the ideas accepted in Marxist circles, deserves careful study especially in the light of the experiences of socialist economies.

[7] In order to stress my point about the change in the nature of the relationship between the base and the superstructure under socialism I have purposely omitted any discussion of the possible ways in which the transition from capitalism to socialism may be made.

framework. Nor does my assertion about the relationship between base and superstructure invalidate the general theses of historical materialism. In stressing the fact that the Marxist definition of the socialist relations of production *must contain within itself* a *political* definition of the state, I wish only to point out that, under socialism, economic and political factors are inseparable. Unless we realize the nature of this truly dialectical *unity* we shall be unable to make a deeper analysis of the processes to be found in a socialist system, especially—and this is the direct concern of economists—economic processes.

## The nature of social ownership. The socialization of the means of production as a process

The inseparability of the economic and political factors becomes quite clear as soon as a closer examination of the term 'social ownership' is undertaken.

Ownership means that the object owned is disposed of *by* the owner in his own interests (broadly conceived). For ownership to be social, therefore, it must satisfy two criteria: the disposition of the object owned must be *in the interest of society* and the owned object must be disposed of *by society*.

Is the first criterion not sufficient? Is it not possible to imagine a paternalistic system in which the interests of the masses are realized by a small *avant garde* without the participation of society in decisions about the way in which the means of production are employed? Especially as far as the long run is concerned, I think that the answer to this question must be 'no'. The longer the period of time that separates a socialist society from its point of departure, from its revolutionary origin, the determination of what is and what is not in the social interest becomes more and more difficult without the activization and extension of a democratic mechanism through which society can participate in the government of the state, i.e., in deciding how resources are to be allocated. Means are always limited—rival goals, none of them at first sight, taken singly, against the social interest, are very numerous. Choosing between these alternatives, ordering them according to scale, timing, etc., unless there is an appropriate mechanism for social initiative in verification and control, is increasingly likely to lead to arbitrariness. This in turn may lead to:

1. objective errors, decisions which do not coincide with the social interest;

2. undesirable subjective effects with regard to whether and how the social interest is realized.

This is, therefore, a further reason for believing that the two criteria cannot be separated. Thus, without also applying them jointly, no progress can be expected in overcoming the alienation of the worker from the means and purposes of his labour. And the problem of overcoming alienation is the fundamental issue in the evolution of the socialist socio-economic system, if it is really to develop towards 'a community of free individuals, carrying on their work with the means of production in common, in which the labour-power of all the different individuals is consciously applied as the combined labour-power of the community'.[8]

If we agree with the proposition that an economy based on social ownership in the full meaning of this word entails the realization of the two criteria set out above and the corresponding reflection of this fact in the consciousness of people, then, albeit only for this reason (omitting other questions as, for example, the question of the material-technical base), we should, in order to be consistent, recognize that *the socialization of the means of production is a process* and not a once-for-all act. For it is clear that both our criteria for the social character of ownership cannot be completely realized in one fell swoop. The nationalization of the means of production in the course of a revolution is undoubtedly the critical step on the path to overcoming alienation but it is, none the less, only the first, and not the last, step in a long and complicated process in which the fundamental role is played by the increasingly comprehensive influence of society on the way in which the nationalized means of production are deployed.

The concept of the socialization of the means of production as a process contains also the idea that this process may not be understood as tending automatically in a particular direction. In certain circumstances to which we shall refer later, it may even be regressive.

[8] Karl Marx, *Capital*, Moscow, 1965, vol. 1, p. 78.

The concept which we have elaborated may also be used to provide a rational interpretation of the idea of the expanded reproduction of socialist relations of production, an idea which forms an inseparable part of the Marxist theory of reproduction.[9] In the political economy of socialism we normally restrict ourselves to the assertion that the expanded reproduction of the socialist means of production consists in the expansion of the *scope*, the increase in the specific gravity of state ownership (or of state and co-operative ownership in the transitional period from capitalism to socialism). This is, however, to simplify the problem. The expanded reproduction of the socialist relations of production consists not only in increasing the scope of state ownership (which, in any case, has an absolute limit), but also and above all in *deepening* its social character—a development connected with the whole of the economic relations between people in a socialist system.

## Two arguments denying that socialization is a process

The proposition that socialization is a process is not new. Some of its elements may be found in Lenin, who, in his pamphlet, *The Immediate Tasks of the Soviet Government*, differentiated between the confiscation of capitalist property and its actual socialization. At the beginning of the 1920s this problem made its appearance several times in different forms only to vanish later—like many other issues. Recently, in the Polish literature, the idea of socialization as a process has emerged again, mainly in a philosophical and sociological context (alienation) but also in connection with economics.

However, it is clear that the analysis of the *process* of the socialization of the means of production is still in its initial stages. This is one, although not, of course, the only reason for the persistence of views denying that socialization is a process. Two kinds of argument based on opposing assumptions and leading to extremely different conclusions may be distinguished.

[9] 'It is not only the actual conditions of the production process which are its result, but also their *specific social character;* social relations, the social structure in which individuals engaged in economic activity find themselves mutually related and the *production relations* as such—are themselves created and are the constantly renewed result of the process.' *Arkhiv Marksa,* Moscow, 1933, p. 166.

*The first argument* consists in treating state ownership in present conditions as, fundamentally, a mature form of social ownership. The supporters of this view start from the sound belief that socialist state ownership is the opposite of capitalist ownership and they emphasize the fact that socialist state ownership arose from the revolutionary overthrow of capitalism. Fundamentally this argument holds that the problem of socialization is resolved by nationalization and the organization of a planned economy. The problem of the political forms needed for the realization of the social interest and for the influence of society on economic decision is either ignored or else considered to be catered for *ex definitione* by the existing system of political institutions. Development is understood only as the evolution of *forms* of ownership (the assimilation of state and co-operative ownership, changes in the organization of state ownership, etc.).

The argument that the socialization of the means of production is something which has been achieved once and for all constitutes a sort of fetishism of the relations of production. From time to time this fetishism shows itself when severe criticisms of the state of the economy and the system of economic relationships in a particular period are made; these criticisms have always been made, so far, *ex post*, immediately after some major change in the upper levels of the political structure. At such times the undesirable consequences of denying, or failing to see, the *objective need* for pushing ahead with the process of socialization make themselves very obvious. These consequences are felt in every field of social life, most strongly in the economy, and especially in the feeling that the connection between personal and social interests on the one hand and participation in the deployment of the means of production on the other is insufficient. These phenomena are too obvious to escape attention. However, when studied, too often it is declared that they are the result of subjective errors and capitalist survivals in the consciousness of people. This interpretation also implies that the extent of these undesirable phenomena will diminish with the passage of time and that there is no need to provide solutions to the continual reappearance of such socio-economic conflicts, which still arise despite the completely new social framework. The problem of capitalist survivals in the consciousness of people is treated as God treated Moses, who was ordered to wander for forty years in the wilderness so that no one who had 'come out of the House of Bondage' should reach the Promised Land. The appositeness of the biblical example is, however, doubtful, since much of what some stubbornly describe as 'capitalist survivals in the consciousness' are the result of current social experience. Moreover, the undesirable phenomena may intensify with the passage of time. I think that there are two reasons for the appearance of this danger:

1. a combination of administrative pressure and political appeals, based on a certain amount of credit extended by public opinion, is effective only in the short term. In the long run it is necessary to establish a continuous, systematic and active attitude to work and to the nationalized means of production; inadequate progress in creating a sense of real participation in economic management makes itself increasingly strongly felt.

2. with the passage of time, new occasions for social conflict make their appearance. Immediately after the revolutionary overthrow of capitalism an extensive and rapid structural change takes place. The new social structure is still liquid; social mobility—mainly because of the massive emancipation of people from classes and strata hitherto oppressed—is very great. After a certain time, however, new social divisions and stratification begin to harden, and inequalities in the standard of living (to some extent, the inevitable result of the system of incentives) begin to threaten what we call 'equality of opportunity'. In these circumstances the need for a conscious and broad participation in the determination of the economic programme, *together with its social consequences*, the need for a thorough public discussion of the various alternatives, becomes especially acute. If this need is not fulfilled, the broad masses of society, and especially the working class, not only fail to raise the level of their political consciousness, but, on the contrary, lose their ability to understand the true sources of the difficulties and tend to place the responsibility for failure on the system as such instead of attributing it to the imperfection of the instruments through which it operates. It is clear that this can give rise to a cumulative process in which the sense of the connection between personal and social interests is weakened.

All this demonstrates only too clearly the significance of the problem of socialization *as a process* and the danger of closing our eyes to it.

*The second argument* against the acceptance of socialization as a process consists in denying that the existing system of state ownership displays any of the features of social ownership. In support of this argument reference is made to those elements in the socio-economic real world which show most clearly the incomplete character of the socialization of the means of production (contradictions between personal and social interests, both short and long term; the existence of a distinct state apparatus deploying the means of production in the name of society without a sufficiently developed political system to guarantee the real influence of society on the way in which they are used; an inequality in incomes and more or less camouflaged privileges greater than would be required by a rational system of incentives, etc.). Hence, like the first argument, the second view is based not so much on the falsification of reality (although this is not to be excluded) as on a flagrantly one-sided approach, considering some aspects to the exclusion of all others, and on the static character of its assumptions and conclusions.

The most extreme example of the denial that the means of production have been socialized in socialist countries is to be found in Djilas's idea of the 'new class'. In asserting that there has been no socialization of the means of production in socialist countries but only the replacement of one exploiting class by another ('the central political bureaucracy'), Djilas is by no means original, but simply repeats—in general, less successfully—ideas formulated in the past by participants in the revolutionary movement, disillusioned because the overthrow of capitalism failed to produce at a stroke a new society founded exclusively on the free union of free people. None the less, views like those of Djilas have been echoed, especially among young people. This would indicate that they are not without foundation. Support for them arises partly, perhaps, as a result of youth's failure to find satisfactory answers to a series of questions with which they have been presented by life. It is no accident that the idea of a 'new class' has found a response precisely among those young people who were brought up in Marxist traditions and who took the idea of socialism for their own. What we have here is a peculiar kind of vulgarization of Marxism resulting from the inadequacy of the Marxist analysis of the relations of production under socialism. For a long time socialism was portrayed in the orthodox Marxist literature as being conflictless; today the situation has undergone a considerable change but the recognition of the existence of conflicts is often still only lip-service or else limited to secondary issues. Reality, however, supplies only too many examples of conflicts both acute and deep. In the absence of other analytical instruments young adepts of Marxism sometimes try to classify these conflicts by employing the categories which Marxism developed for capitalism. This, I think, is one of the basic reasons for the ill-considered views which deny that socialization is a process and which offer a primitive description of the nationalized means of production as simply the property of 'the central political bureaucracy', which is supposed to exploit society in its own immediate interest.

This is not the place to make a full critique of this attitude. I would like only to note that if the conception of a 'new class' is to be taken literally then this class of 'the central political bureaucracy' would be perhaps the smallest exploiting class in history and one, moreover, which had developed at lightning speed in the course of a few years. At the same time this tiny ruling class, which has developed so speedily, has at its disposal an enormous quantity of productive forces concentrated on an unprecedented scale. If we accept Djilas's thesis that the aim of this 'new class' is its own material advantage, one would expect that the members of this class would have an unusually high level of income and that there would be an enormous difference between their incomes and those of other social strata. Taking all elements of income into account, formal and informal, there is no evidence for this.

This does not mean that there were or are not examples of the acquisition of excessively privileged material positions by members of ruling groups. But this is a long way from a 'new class'—using the word in Marx's sense—a class exploiting an enormous productive apparatus in order to appropriate surplus value for its own economic advantage. Djilas's conception of a 'new class' is scientifically sterile both as it stands and even as a very general hypothesis. This

95

conception adds nothing to our knowledge of the socio-economic processes in socialism, because:

1. it is unhistorical—it completely disregards the connection between the origin of a system, the socio-economic and political preconditions and the motor forces which gave rise to it on the one hand, and the processes of its further development on the other;

2. it is subjectivist—no attempt is made to cite objective reasons for the transformation of yesterday's revolutionaries into today's exploiters, just as nothing—except faith—is offered as a justification for the gamble that all conflicts may be resolved by overthrowing the 'new class'.

Thus the first argument, denying that socialization is a process, is really the fetishism of the overthrow of the political and economic rule of the *bourgeoisie*. This is to fail to see that the essence of socialist development depends, and must depend, not only on the creation of a material base, but also, and perhaps primarily, on the difficult and complex task of developing the socio-political factors necessary for the development of the socialization of the means of production.

The second argument against treating socialization as a process ignores the fact that the nationalization of the means of production and the revolutionary transformation of the social structure create what are in principle the *objective preconditions* for socialization and give rise to qualitative changes. The full socialization of ownership and the conquest of alienation will be achieved, not through a 'second socio-economic revolution', but by working for the further development of the revolution which has already taken place.

It is difficult to accept that any of these concepts has helped to provide a deeper analysis of social ownership as the basis of socialist relations of production.

## The objective character of the difficulties in the process of socialization

So far our arguments have tended to show that the socialization of ownership cannot be completed at one stroke and that it is not simply a function of the passage of time. Progress in this field requires that a whole series of difficulties should be overcome. These difficulties arise *objectively* in *every* socialist country although in some countries (because of their low level of economic development, lack of democratic traditions, etc.), these difficulties may constitute a particularly formidable impediment to the socialization of ownership. The correct approach to the development of socialist relations of production ought, therefore, to start with a recognition of the objective nature of the impediments to it, studying them and showing how they can be removed.

The germs of this approach can be found in Marxist literature. One of the first was sketched in an article by Rosa Luxemburg in her pamphlet about the Russian revolution. Rosa Luxemburg, unlike the theorists of the 'new class', did not assume that the ruling élite were motivated by egoism or that their purpose was to appropriate social surplus value to themselves. On the contrary, she accepted that the political leaders were subjectively moved by almost unlimited altruism and great idealism. Nevertheless, working on these correct assumptions, she did not exclude the possibility of a divergence between this activity and the interest and will of the working masses. She saw the real danger of bureaucracy, of serious social conflicts and of the weakening of the revolutionary impetus if the objectively necessary process of creating a specific governmental and economic apparatus did not go hand in hand with a persistent and effective struggle for increasing the real participation of society in the disposition of the means of production and output.

During the October Revolution and the Civil War, Lenin did not see these as such important problems; a fact to be explained by the nature of the revolutionary achievements and the widespread spontaneous democratic spirit characteristic of this period of great transformations. It only needed, however, a short period of relative stability for Lenin clearly to perceive the danger of bureaucracy, as the articles and notes of the last months of his life show all too starkly. No concrete programme of solutions is to be found in these writings but everyone must be struck by the growing consciousness that what is needed for the successful development of the socialist system is the fullest participation of the mass of the people in the management of the state. If there is anything which can be described as Lenin's testament it is to be found in these articles and notes, hastily composed in the shadow of death, in which he stresses the need to fight the objective threat of bureaucracy—the alienation of the apparatus of government, its transformation from the people's tool into a force standing over the people.

Today a whole epoch has left us much richer in experience. Nowadays we more readily realize that the growth of the apparatus of economic administration (bureaucratization, in the usual meaning of the term) is not only and not even primarily the result of incompetence but is the specific result of the modern organization of productive forces, the price which society has to pay for the control of processes which have hitherto been spontaneous. The prophecy that economic management would be so simplified that direct management would be possible without the permanent division of labour has not been fulfilled. On the contrary, the mechanism of management has become increasingly complicated and the importance of specialists in various branches of economic life has grown. The differentiation of income by reference to position in the social division of labour and the merging of the political and economic apparatus at high levels has created a situation in which the effective influence of society on economic decisions and an increase in the identification of personal with social interests cannot be regarded as guaranteed *ex definitione*.

The fact that the process of the socialization of the means of production—in the sense in which we use the term—encounters objective difficulties does not invalidate the proposition that the socialist revolution creates the preconditions for overcoming alienation. It does deny the truth of the view, which we have already criticized several times, that progress in this direction is automatic. Hindrances must be effectively countered and one of the main means for doing so is undoubtedly to be found in the proper evolution of the political system. If no action is taken then the process of socialization will slow down or even stop or regress. In the economic sphere, this will be reflected by different forms of under-utilization of the factors of development of a socialist economy. Moreover, the damage resulting from this will affect the growth of people's income. This in turn will adversely affect the feeling of the connection between personal and social interests, as well as shaping the collective attitude towards the management of the nationalized means of production. We may thus be faced with a cumulatively deteriorating situation.

It is not easy to come to positive conclusions about all this. However, the general direction of development is clear; the system for the exercise of state power must evolve so that there is a constant real growth in the influence of society on politico-economic decisions at all levels and an increase in social self-government in all areas of life, especially in economic activities. This is the fundamental sense of the traditional Marxist thesis that the state, as a socially alienated apparatus of coercion, will gradually wither away.[10]

This idea follows consistently, in my opinion, from the analysis of the connection between the base and the superstructure in the socialist system, of the link between the expanded reproduction of the socialist relations of production and the democratic evolution of a system for exercising the power of the state. The concept is obviously a very general one. The study of the concrete stages of its evolution requires the application of techniques drawn from all branches of social science including political science in its strict sense.

I think that the general line which such a study should take in order to be successful can be more clearly defined by enumerating a number of factors which more or less determine the path to be taken.

I consider *the first of these factors* to be the proper appreciation of the significance of the problem itself. It is clear that no one in the socialist countries denies the need for 'further democratization' of social life. Such assertions are nothing more than words unless they are accompanied by a critical evaluation of existing political institutions. The political system must not be fetishized, it must not be allowed to remain a taboo which specialists may not examine if such examination threatens to be more than the formal exegesis of texts; and ordinary mortals, whose interests extend beyond their own private affairs, must be permitted to discuss it. In order better and more fully to realize the rights of society as the owner of the nationalized means of production it is necessary to recognize the limited

[10] 'The more democratic the "state", which consists of the armed workers, and which is "no longer a state in the proper sense of the word", the more rapidly *every form* of state begins to wither away.' V. I. Lenin, *Selected works*, London, 1969, p. 337.

application of certain forms of economic and political life even if those forms were at one time necessary precisely because they were exceptional. 'The Bolsheviks had no choice,' wrote Julian Hochfeld in an article about Rosa Luxemburg's pamphlet, *The Russian Revolution*; 'they were forced to fight for power and take power into their hands if they wanted to forestall the counter-revolution.' The responsibility for the isolation of the October Revolution, as Rosa Luxemburg emphasized, falls not on them but on the social-democratic opportunists. It would be senseless, says Rosa, to demand that Lenin and his comrades should conjure up a beautiful democracy, a model dictatorship of the proletariat or a thriving socialist economy in such conditions. The danger begins only when a virtue is made of necessity and when an attempt is made to create a whole theoretical system out of the tactical achievements dictated by circumstances and when this system is presented to the working-class movement of the whole world as the sacrosanct principle by which their actions should be governed. Before we can make any progress we must, therefore, discard our satisfaction with the existing state of affairs and become aware, not only of the great mass of real achievements which has already been accumulated, but also of the vast number of problems which had to be resolved along the road on which we ourselves are about to set out. Marxists have always correctly resisted the fetishism of political democracy as a substitute for revolutionary social change. This does not, however, justify the neglect of political democracy after the revolution is over and when new socio-economic conditions have taken root.

*The second task* would be to make a full assessment of the part played by changes in the functioning of the economy on the democratization of political and economic life. The increase in the independence of enterprises or of units of local administration which follows from the changes entailed by the 'decentralized model' is of very great importance. These changes create the preconditions for the development of workers' self-government in the lower levels of the economy and generally reduce the concentration of power devoted to 'the administration of things' which, as we know from experience, can easily lead to the ruthless administration of people. None the less, while appreciating the potential importance of this kind of development, it must still be remembered that this is not sufficient and that this will not *by itself* guarantee the necessary speed and scale for the process of socialization. In a planned economy where, irrespective of the model employed, the partial optima must be subordinated to the optimum for the economy as a whole, the actions of individual enterprises and regions must be dependent on the situation in the economy as a whole, on macro-economic decisions. It is not enough if the democratization of the employment of the means of production is restricted to the enterprise or the unit of local administration; indeed, restricting democratization in this way may, in the long run, lead to the intensification of conflicts between the interests of particular groups and the interests of the whole.

Therefore, the realization of the needs of a decentralized model of economic management, in order to be effective both from a purely economic and from a socio-economic point of view, requires that society be given real influence on general decisions. It must be able to influence choices about fundamental problems—the division of the national income at the macro-economic level and especially the formulation of long-term economic plans and their social consequences.

*In the third place* one must be prepared in advance for all the difficulties which accompany the expansion and deepening of the democratization of political and economic life. If, for example, the discussion of the division between investment and consumption, the division of consumption between the private and collective sectors, income differentiation, etc., is thrown open, this may give rise to real problems especially in situations which require decisive action. Autocratic decision-making is not without its advantages. But in general these are only short-term advantages, and entail much greater disadvantages on the long-term. Stanisław Ossowski, the sociologist and social thinker, classifying the types of social order in his book *Osobliwość nauk spolecznych*,[11] wrote that he much preferred 'the conception of a social order . . . designed to reconcile the polycentric nature of social life with rational planning', since 'what has to be resolved is the conflict between the effectiveness of a unified central

[11] *The peculiarities of the social sciences*, Warsaw, 1962.

authority and the humanist values of polycentrism'. I agree with this and think it needs only to be qualified by the observation that, in spite of all the short-term difficulties, in the long term there should be no such conflict in a socialist system where the humanization of the relations between people on the one hand, and economic advance on the other, are interdependent.

In this essay the problems of political economy and the connection between economy and politics in socialism have only been roughly sketched. I have not tried to be systematic and the way in which I have gone about it will probably excite argument and opposition on all sides. One thing is certain; it is vain to expect the application of a programme of *political* economy in the strict sense without the critical development and application of Marxist theory to the socialist system. The dialectical laws of social movement discovered by Marx do not lose their force at the opening of a new epoch and although it is usually difficult to draw lessons from them for one's own society, we must do so—for the sake of its development.

[First published in *Critica Marxista*, no. 1, Rome, 1966.]

# 7 | Contradictions and ways to resolve them

It is now some time since the problems of the 'Polish December' ceased to occupy the front pages of the international press. But it would be harmful for socialism and for the international workers' movement if the important lessons to be learnt from the recent events in Poland were to be lost or obliterated by the passage of time. The risk is not theoretical but real, not only because of the inexorable and universal law whereby impact is lost with the passage of time, but also because of the understandable tendency to forget things which are unpalatable and difficult—and the Polish events are both of these—for communist parties whether in socialist or in non-socialist countries. So, none the less, we must try to analyse these events in a straightforward way which is all the more profound and bold for being free from the emotions of the moment.

## The significance of the working-class demonstrations

The essential and long-term significance of the events in Poland in December 1970 arises from a few simple facts.

1. The demonstrations were genuinely working class—they were carried out by workers in the major industries. The initial attempt of the former Party leadership and the government to pass them off as the work of hooligan and anti-social elements collapsed completely. Since then, no one has dared to deny publicly the truly working-class nature of the demonstrations. Moreover, no one has since sought to link them with the activities of hostile centres either within the country or abroad, nor have there been any serious accusations of revisionism. Leaving aside for the moment the general background of the December 1970 events, it may be said that the *spontaneous* nature of the movement was recognized, although the movement itself, in spite of the situation, had shown a remarkable capacity for rapid and efficient organization—a capacity worthy of the best Polish working-class tradition.

2. The immediate effect of the workers' demonstrations and the tragic bloodshed was the change in the political leadership of the country. Wladyslaw Gomulka and his closest colleagues were forced out of the political arena—those very statesmen who had been responsible for the government of the country for the last fifteen years or so and who, in a sense, symbolized that period.

3. Following the December demonstrations and as a result of the pressure brought to bear by the working class in the succeeding months, the price increases were cancelled—although up to the last moment there were attempts to justify them; the wages and salaries freeze policy, introduced under the pretext of the so-called system of economic incentives, was abandoned, and fundamental changes were made to allow for an increase in consumer goods in the economic plan for 1971, etc.

Taken together, these facts bear witness to the depth and range of the social struggle and contradictions which afflicted Poland. It is no longer a theoretical question of admitting, in an abstract sense, the existence of contradictions within socialist countries, but the concrete and tangible framework of such contradictions, a framework which renders inevitable certain general conclusions. Moreover, if the Marxist method is effectively applied to an analysis of real-life conditions in socialist countries, the conclusions drawn from the Polish events cannot by any means be dismissed as relating only to a personality cult or to errors committed once only. It proves that it is not enough to denounce and condemn, even with the greatest good will, the 'errors and distortions' of the Stalinist period; it is not enough even to make changes, if these changes are only superficial and do not tackle the roots of the problems, or fail to create conditions for a continuing process of adjustment. The politicians who were forced to leave the helm of government in December 1970 had been active in the communist resistance when Poland was occupied by the Nazis: three of them—Gomulka, Kliszko and especially Spychalski—had been persecuted in the Stalinist period. The triumphal return of Władysław Gomułka to the political scene in October 1956 with the slogan, 'No more Poznańs', now assumes almost the scale of a classical tragedy, of a symbol, if one remembers that his inglorious disappearance from the arena after fifteen years in power took place again under even stronger pressure from the workers, and at the price of a greater number of victims. The wheel has turned full circle, although there is no doubt that Gomułka wished to avoid a repetition of the Poznań experience and was fully convinced that he was doing his utmost towards that end.

The conclusion is so obvious that there is no need to spell it out. In the present government system in Poland (which does not appear to differ substantially from those in other East European socialist countries) there must be factors due to which social and economic contradictions have not been solved. On the contrary, these were concealed, so that they ultimately exploded with even greater force. As a Marxist, I think that it is only in these terms that we can explain to ourselves and to others the causes of the tragic events and the paradoxical fate of some of the outstanding personalities in the Polish working-class movement.

## An attempt to define the causes of the crisis

An exhaustive answer to the question of why these suppressed contradictions grew to the point of explosion would doubtless need much analysis. And the freer the climate of true investigation, the more effective the analysis—the orthodox systems of thinking and explanation will no longer serve. The following attempt is, by its nature, open to discussion.

The direct causes of the workers' demonstrations of December 1970 in Poland were economic difficulties and the attempt to overcome them at the expense of the proletariat. But what was the cause of these economic difficulties and of the positive choice of this and not some other means to overcome them?

The author considers that the basic causes of the trouble lay in the *political* system. This assertion should not be considered surprising since, in a socialist country—where most of the means of production are nationalized and the state controls the entire economy on the basis of central economic planning—the system of political power and methods of government become indivisible and perhaps a central feature in the network of relations of production. Without analysing these features and the extent to which the working class really participates in the exercise of power, it is impossible to define the true character of the ownership of the means of production, and it is the latter which decides the nature of every system of the relations of production. It is therefore only to be expected that, in these conditions, the classic Marxist law of development through revealing and overcoming the contradictions between the need for the development of productive forces and the nature of the production relations should find expression in contradictions between the needs of the economy and the political system. It does not seem too hard to test this theory; let us restrict ourselves to the Polish experience of the last few years.

It is well known that the modern theory of decision-making attaches great importance to the existence of preconditions for a swift, free and—most important—as far as possible unbiased *flow of information*. This becomes increasingly significant, the greater the importance of the decision and the effect of its results. From this point of view it is indeed surprising to observe the limited range as well as the degree of distortion of the information available to the previous leadership of the Polish United Workers' Party when it decided to increase food prices in December 1970, just before the Christmas festivities. To judge from the pronouncements made after the December events, the Party leadership was in the dark not only about the true economic situation but also about current political opinion both in large sections of the working class and in the upper ranks of the Party and government. It has been discovered that those responsible for making decisions were not up to date with the actual situation. From articles published after the December events it is clear that members of the Central Committee, of the government, of the trade unions, and even members of the Politbureau and the Secretariat of the Central Committee were highly critical—some dramatically so—of the actions being prepared. Nevertheless, there is no proof of any attempt to go back on these decisions; no proof of any energetic opposition to them. It is not a matter of making personal assessments or judgments of politicians for not having resisted them in time; the problem lies with the system whereby it becomes a rule not to tell a superior the truth but to give him such information as may be in line with his own point of view, whether expressed or presumed.

The total blockade of the flow of information—all the more incomprehensible to anyone not involved—which occurred in Poland in December 1970 was the culmination of what had been happening over many years. Inevitably, experience taught that, from a personal point of view, toeing the Party line yielded benefits— while criticism brought personal troubles—regardless of the real social results. As for the economic sector, one of the most typical examples of this was the abortive attempt *to discuss the proposed five-year economic plan for the years 1966–70*; its implementation led among other things to the tragic result of December 1970. The plan, as far as agricultural policy and foreign trade in agricultural products in particular was concerned, contained concepts which aroused great concern as well as the opposition of certain economists worried by the possible drop in meat production and thus in the people's standard of living. This happened in 1964, during the period of public discussion officially announced before the IV Congress of the Polish United Workers' Party. There were attempts to express reservations in public—none of which was concerned with fundamental socialist principles but all with certain concrete answers to problems of economic policy. One of the best known and internationally respected Polish economists expressed his point of view in writing; not restricting himself to criticism he went further, proposing alternative concrete solutions. The Party leadership immediately took exceptionally violent action against him. Every attempt at practical discussion was immediately quashed, and at no time would the Party— including the Congress—even consider the possibility of examining the proposed alternative. After this experience, no hope remained of any allowance for independent economic assessment or analysis.

In a sense, the whole history of the last fifteen years of abortive attempts to bring about economic reform in Poland can serve as an example of the destructive influence of the present political system on economic processes. It goes without saying that economic reform cannot be considered as the panacea for all economic difficulties, but even within these limits to put it into operation would doubtless be very beneficial. This is particularly true of a country such as Poland, which must rely primarily on mobilizing intensive sources of development: increase in productivity, adjusting the pattern of 'product mix' to demand, more effective deployment of resources, improvements in investment processes, etc. Poland was among the first socialist countries to work out advanced plans for economic reform, for the first steps to bring them about were being taken soon after October 1956. These plans received the formal approval of the highest political authorities who, in their stated programmes, repeatedly asserted their wish to bring them into effect. But the fact remains that nothing was done, chiefly because of the fear that reforms might possibly put some limits to the autocracy and high-handedness of the political authorities. The attempt to correlate changes in the economic system with the growth of workers' self-management was regarded with particular disfavour. The workers' councils, which grew up spontaneously in factories during the 'Polish October', were reduced almost to a purely formal role, and they completely lost all characteristics of a true representative workers' body in the management of the economy. In 1970 the former leadership of the Polish United Workers' Party sought to exploit the ideas of reform in order to conceal a rigid deflationary policy, aiming at a virtual freeze of wages and salaries for a minimum period of two years. The so-called new system of economic incentives which was to have come into effect at the beginning of 1971—cancelled after 20 December 1970—had thus only succeeded in discrediting the idea of economic reform in the eyes of public opinion.

The examples quoted are concerned with problems linked, directly or indirectly, to the economic causes of the events of the few months immediately before December 1970. They have however a more general significance, clearly showing the braking effect of a faulty political system on the development of the forces of production and on social relations. It is worth bearing in mind, particularly in the age of the so-called information revolution, that to build a comprehensive information system, in the broadest sense, requires not only modern *technical* solutions but also adequate *political* conditions.

## The workers' demonstrations and the situation in intellectual circles

The contradiction between the requirements of economic development and an inadequate political system is not static, but of a dynamic character; it can be resolved only by adjusting and democratizing the system. It is therefore relevant to an understanding of the events of December 1970 to refer to the events of March 1968.

First, however, I should warn the reader not to seek superficial analogies, for they do not exist, between demonstrations in intellectual (particularly student) circles in the West and in Poland. The causes of demonstrations in the West and in Poland were rooted in the prevailing specific conditions and, therefore, were not of the same character. In Poland in 1968 the protests of a great number of students and intellectuals was an expression of their increasing consciousness of the self-retarding nature of the process of development of the political system. They saw this process as distinct both from the socialist ideals of the freedom of the individual and from the sheer pragmatic requirements of social and economic development mentioned above. The issues at the core of the protests were the demand for the re-establishment of fundamental civil liberties and, most important, the abandonment of the practice of distortion and withholding of information. At the same time, clearly, there was no question of undermining the foundations of the socialist regime; rather, the intention was to shield it from the tumult that was bound to ensue from political backwardness. The students' March 1968 slogan, 'There is no bread without liberty', expressed the basic links between economy and politics in a socialist country. December 1970 provided urgent confirmation of this, in a most agonizing way.

The response of the then Polish leaders was a decision which had most unfortunate consequences. It was decided to exploit the demonstrations of the students and intellectuals by annihilating once and for all every source, actual or potential, of independent criticism. As frequently happens in such circumstances, it was evidently believed that the trouble sprang not out of real contradictions but rather out of attempts, albeit minimal, to speak aloud the unvarnished truth.

The plan was carried out by a wide range of means, starting with exceptionally brutal and repressive police measures, going so far as to use the monopoly of the mass media to warp completely the real nature and intentions of the student and intellectual demonstrations. I do not propose to give here a profound analysis of the methods used, but I must say that notes were struck in the ideological campaign which had never been heard before, on such a large scale and so openly, even in the darkest days of the Stalinist purges. (Here one thinks first of the so-called anti-Zionist campaign, which was generally interpreted in Poland as a blow consciously directed against the relatively few politically active Poles of Jewish origin.) As a result they succeeded not only in removing from the public scene all those directly charged with criticism of the existing state of affairs, but they also succeeded in intimidating all intellectual groups. To some extent, thanks to this ideological campaign just described, they even succeeded in driving a wedge between the working class and the protesting students and intellectuals.

In the light of subsequent events it may be said that they succeeded in obtaining results in line with those they wanted, in that in December 1970 the intellectuals—and in particular their official representatives—kept silent, even at the most dramatic moments. Hopefully, this fact does not seem destined to form part of the glorious heritage of socialism. But another fact did have very great importance, in that since March 1968 no critical voice has made itself heard condemning the policies—particularly the economic policies—of the leadership of the country of the time, even though, as is admitted today both generally and officially, decisions were frequently incorrect and arbitrary. The connection between this lack of criticism and the extent of the mistaken and high-handed decisions is evident. The success of the measures adopted in March 1968 gave those who devised them and benefited from them the feeling that they had absolute liberty to act autocratically, which eventually led to the events of December 1970. In this lies the real link between March 1968 and December 1970, a link which may be taken as a classic example, even if a negative one, of the dialectic character of the processes of social development: to suppress the outward manifestations of contradictions without effectively overcoming their causes will of itself create sources of still sharper contradictions, and will multiply the strength, the range and the dangerous effects of the delayed explosion. Indeed, from the point of view of social and political dangers, what did the demonstrations of young students, a few writers and scholars in March 1968 amount to, compared with the demonstrations of the large-scale industrial proletariat in a chain of important Polish economic centres in December 1970? It is indeed difficult to overestimate the significance of this concrete lesson in dialectical and historical materialism.

There is a frequent attempt to deny the interdependence of political and economic factors in the development of the recent events, and simply to indicate the apparently purely economic character of the workers' demands. The reasoning does not appear to be justified. First: granted that the requests has a purely economic nature, there remains undisputed the theory of interdependence between economic and political factors in bringing about the situation which gave rise to the demonstrations. Second, the workers' demands were concerned, directly and indirectly, with important political problems, although they were not, perhaps, given sufficiently general expression. (This, I think, was due to the lack of co-operation between the workers and the students and intellectuals; although on the other hand one must ask whether, in the actual situation, this fact did not have advantageous results.) The demands were primarily concerned with democratization of relations at factory level, changing the nature of elections in certain organizations, including that of the Party, true autonomy and a new approach in the trades unions, publicizing information without distortion, an effective fight against bureaucracy, the abolition of privilege of position, of types of non-public organization, etc. In the economic sphere, demands to increase the autonomy of the enterprises were fairly numerous. These demands were doubly significant: as foundations for a wider and more effective use of production capacities and as the basis for real, not fictitious, workers' self-government. Examining these requests with great care, one cannot escape their wider political significance. From this point of view the Polish working class has proved its own maturity precisely in its understanding of the connections between economy and politics in socialism, showing moreover a good sense of reality regarding the extent and method of advancing its demands.

## To benefit fully from experience

The fact that the workers' demonstrations led to a change in the political leadership in Poland is in itself of value, if rightly interpreted.

The problem is that the change of politicians ought to be considered as the beginning and not the end of a process, as an opening-up of *possibilities* for the solution of contradictions when the time is ripe, and not as the solution itself. A series of measures immediately taken by the present government, particularly in the economic field, would seem to be a move in the right direction: it is obvious, however, that it is not a question of immediate, but of long-term, action, to cure not the symptoms but the basic causes. This is not the place for a detailed analysis of the elements of a vast and courageous programme which should indeed transform possibilities into reality. Such a programme is, on the contrary, the result of a critical analysis of the causes of the crisis.

To draw up an adequate programme one must of course take into account the characters of the Party and government leaders, the extent to which they understand the causes of the trouble and also the extent to which they are ready and willing to effect the necessary changes. But do not let us delude ourselves. To carry them into effect will arouse the opposition of the forces of conservatism, accustomed as they are to act repressively rather than in the manner appropriate to the present political situation, i.e., to ensure the wider participation of workers in the solution of major problems, present and future. It is for this reason that it seems so important to remove everything which, in the recent past, made it impossible to adopt and to express freely a critical attitude to problems which concern the whole of society and which, in a socialist regime, should be the concern of everyone; otherwise the people would continue to feel powerless and unable to influence the decisions taken in their name.

One particularly important lesson to draw from the experience of December 1970 and from the succeeding period is to realise that even in a socialist system, the adaptation of the relations of production to the demands of development of the forces of production does not happen automatically, but in the course of active social processes. And its result depends not so much on the good will of individuals (although as we have stressed above this is not a negligible aspect) as on the relevant balance of social forces. It is from this angle that one must judge the significance of social pressure in Poland which we see, a pressure exercised in the first place by the working class. We are accustomed to consider such phenomena in a socialist country as deplorable, to be eliminated at whatever cost and by whatever means; and if it is not possible to eliminate the causes, then at least to eliminate the effects, burying them as deep as possible. I think that it is high time to put an end to these narrow-minded attitudes which basically imply only a loss of faith in the power and the wisdom of the working class. These attitudes express a view which in practice denies to the working class that which the textbooks lay down, namely the political role of the vanguard. In the December 1970 demonstrations, the Polish working class gave a positive example of the role which it develops, and which it must develop, not only in exceptional situations but daily, by means of a strong and steady pressure on those who govern. Only thus will the internal forces in the Party which indeed want to introduce real changes win the social support necessary to the devising and effecting of a plan of action, suited to the needs and the opportunities of socialism. It is unnecessary to stress that the vanguard role of the working class not only does not exclude but on the contrary presupposes an active support from other social groups, and from the intellectuals in particular.

Finally a few reflections on the conclusions arising from the Polish events for the international communist movement. Whether we like it or not, the fact is this: the communist parties and workers in non-socialist countries, and in the developed countries of the West in particular, are considered responsible for what happens in the socialist countries. Even this by itself implies, or rather requires, that communist parties and workers operating outside the socialist countries have an obligation to make an independent analysis of what takes place inside socialist countries; it imposes the *political necessity* that they should adopt an active role in that connection. This appears all the more necessary in that the multiple conclusions drawn from the actual experience of socialist countries shall serve to help them to draw up their own programme, their own strategy, their own view of socialism. It is neither right nor acceptable that the enemies of socialism should have the monopoly of criticizing the socialist world, since they, through force of circumstances, will interpret the reality of the socialist countries in a biased way. It would therefore seem that a critical *but communist* analysis of the experiences of socialism, the renunciation of those analyses which seek only to flatter, is essential not only for the international communist movement but also for the future of world socialism.

[First published in *Rinascita*, Rome, June 1971.]

# Index

Wlodzimierz Brus was born near Warsaw in 1921. During a distinguished career he has held many posts, including that of Director of the Research Bureau of the Planning Commission and Vice-Chairman of the Economic Council (advisory body to the Polish government). He has also been a member of the Polish United Workers' Party. Professor Brus was Professor of Political Economy at the University of Warsaw until 1968, when he was dismissed from his position under accusations of revisionism and 'ideological support' to the students' and intellectuals' revolt. He was then a research worker in the Institute of Housing, Warsaw. Professor Brus is now Visiting Senior Research Fellow in the Department of International Economic Studies, University of Glasgow. He is the author of *The Market in a Socialist Economy* (Routledge & Kegan Paul, 1972).